Elements of Nepalese Temple Architecture

Purusottam Dangol

Elements of Nepalese Temple Architecture

IInd Revised Edition

Purusottam Dangol

ADROIT

Published by
ADROIT PUBLISHERS
4675/21, Ganpati Bhawan, Ansari Road,
Daryaganj, New Delhi-110 002 Phones :
011-23266030, 43598466

Distributors
Akhil Book Distributors
e-mail: akhilbooks@yahoo.com
adroitpublishers@gmail.com

ISBN : 81-87392-77-0

Printed in India on behalf of M/s Adroit Publishers by
M.S. Indian Enterprises, E-mail : msindianbooks@gmail.com

नमः अष्ट मातृका देव्यै

ब्रम्हायणी पीतवर्णाभा कमण्डलु घरं शुभाम् ।
वेदमाता विशालाक्षी नमामि हंस बाहिनीमे ॥1 ॥

रौद्रायणी श्रेतवर्णाभा त्रिशूल पात्र धारिनीम् ।
त्रिनेत्रा चारु वदना नमापि वृष बाहिनीम् ॥2 ॥

इन्द्रायणी कुम्कूमाङ्गी बज्रहस्ता सूरेश्वरीम् ।
सहम् नयना सौम्यां नमामि गजबाहिनीम् ॥3 ॥

बाराही रक्तवर्णाभा मीनाङकूश धराशूभाम् ।
घनघोर कोलास्वा नमामि महिष बाहिनीम् ॥4 ॥

कौमारी रक्तवर्णाभा शक्ति हस्ता भयानकीम् ।
त्रिनेत्रा योवनां गीच नमामि शिखबाहिनीम् ॥5 ॥

वैष्णवी श्यामवर्णाभा चक्रहस्ता मनोहराम् ।
त्रिनेत्रा सौम्य बदनां नमामि गरुड बाहिनीम् ॥6 ॥

चामूण्डा रक्तवर्णाभा खड्ग फेटक धारिनीम् ।
कृष्णाङ्गीक्रोध रुपाचानमामि प्रेतबाहिनीम् ॥7 ॥

महालक्ष्मी श्वेतवर्णा कपाल खड्ग धारिनीम् ।
त्रिनेत्रा सौम्य वदनां नमामिसिंह बाहिनीम् ॥8 ॥

अष्ट क्षत्रे स्थितादेवी अष्ट वृक्ष निवासिनीम् ।
अष्ट भैरव संयुक्तं अष्ट मातृकां नमस्तुते ॥9 ॥

असिताङ्ग प्रचण्डं च रुरुकं कपिलं तथा ।
क्रोध उन्मत्त संहारं भीपम भैरव नमः ॥10 ॥

गणनां गणपति श्रैव गज वक्तं त्रिलोचनं ।
परशु मोदक हस्तं च गणपति नमोस्तुते ॥11 ॥

वीर विक्रम सौन्दयूर्यं शक्ति हस्तन्तु षट्मुखम् ।
सर्व सिद्धि प्रदातारं कुमार प्रनमाम्यऽहम् ॥12 ॥

स्वस्थानं स्वधिकारं च स्वस्वरूप स्व वीजजम् ।
स्वम्व काष्ट वितानं च दिव्याना कुञ्ज भूमिकम् ॥13 ॥

दश दिशु क्षत्रपालं क्षत्राश्रैव त्रयोदश ।
पञ्चा शत क्षत्रपालाश्र पालं नमस्तुते ॥14 ॥

Astra Matrika
Source : Mother-Goddesses in Kathmandu

प्रमाणे स्थापिता देवाः पूजार्हाश्च भवन्ति हि ।

"When the gods are set up with correct proportions then they can be worshipped."

'Samarāṅgaṇasūtradhāra', XL. 13½.

पाचकः कटुतीक्ष्णाद्यैरनुसाररसैर्यथा ॥
अन्वीक्ष्य विपचेत् तद्वत् स्थपतिः सर्वमाचरेत् ।
यदुक्तं यदनुक्तं च तत् समग्रमपि स्फुटम् ॥

"As a cook cooks after testing various suitable flavours, the piquant, the sharp, etc., so should also the architect observe everything; whether stated explicitly or not, all (that is required) is clear (to him)."

ib., LV. 158b—159.

Preface

The magnificent temples of Kathmandu Valley clearly depict the outstanding development of craftsmanship in the field of wood, metal and stone during the Lichchavi and Malla period. These temples have historical, religious, cultural and economic significance as it contributes to local economy through tourism promotion. In fact, Nepal is known throughout the world as a kingdom full of innumerable temples dedicated to different gods and goddesses. Although these temples vary one from another in terms of size and shape but they are all based on certain religious principles and values as well as architectural norms of ancient times. It is widely believed that temples which do not heed to such principles will not deliver the expected benefits. It is also equally interesting to observe the precision in the construction of the temples despite the absence of sophisticated tools and equipments in the past. The traditional unique technology of the ancient period which enabled such construction needs to be studied and preserved. And this could be the potential area of research for future.

Against this backdrop, the conservation of these temples hardly needs any further justifications. Some of these temples have already been included in the World Heritage Site such as the temple of Changu Narayan and Pashupati Nath. Therefore, the inclusion of these temples in the World Heritage Site further necessitates the need for their conservation and preservation of our own national identity and culture.

The studies on temple architecture are comparatively very few therefore an attempt has been made in this book to describe all the important elements of temple in detail as far as possible. Moreover, while describing each element, an effort has also been made to familiarize the readers with traditional way of constructing the temples as well as cited relevant manuscripts whenever possible for further study and research.

It is expected that this book will be of great interest and use not only to the architects and technicians but also to the general readers interested in the study of temple architecture.

I am grateful to Adroit Publisher, in particular, Mr. D.K. Sharma, for kindly undertaking the burden of publication of this book. I would like to express my sincere gratitude to Mr. Dibyeswar Prasad Shrestha, Senior Economist, Department of Urban Development and Building Construction, for his moral support and help.

Finally, I would also like to extend my heartfelt thanks to Mr. Gauri Shankar Dongol, Mr. Ramesh Sthapit, Mr. Raja Shakya and Mr. Sarad Kasa for their help in the completion of this book in an efficient manner.

Ar. Purusottam Dangol

Contents

List of Plates

List of Figures

Chapter 1

Introduction

Nepal is a nation of different races and ethnic groups with their own tradition and religious faith. The devotional faith of the rulers and the people as well as the creative quality of the artisans established a tradition of constructing temples in Nepal. The origin of temples is yet unknown. An inscription dating back to 625 A.D. of Amsuvarma in Sundhara of Patan, refers to the construction of temples with brick and wood. The details of its parts and building material implies to a tier style. The Chinese traveller Wang-Huan-Tsa who visited Nepal in the middle of the 7th century also mentioned the presence of several buildings with multiple roofs in the annals of Tang Dynasty. However the legend suggests that the oldest temple built in Nepal in this style is the Pashupati Nath[1] temple. According to Karpatrick (1811) it was built by the fourth prince of Suryavanshi Dynasty and dedicated to Pashupati Mahadev in the 4th century.

In Nepal any type of temple made out of brick or stone, of any shape, single or multi - tiered roof is called 'mandir'. While in newari (the language of craftsmen) the term 'degah' is used. This term is used for both Hindu and Buddhist religious temples. The other three basic types of temple found in Nepal, independent of the tiered roof, are the stupa, the shikara, and the dome temple.

The scope of this book is limited to the tiered roof temple or, as the westerners calls it the pagoda style temple. However, the term pagoda is commonly used by foreigners as well as Nepalese nowadays. The pagodas of China and Japan are different from Nepalese tiered temples. After doing extensive, comparative work in these areas, Ronald Bernier shows two clear major structural differences. The first of these distinctions, found in pagodas of the Far East regions, but absent in all Nepalese temples, is construction around a central pole which serves as a structural axis. The second is the means of supporting the tiered roofs. In Nepal this problem is solved by the use of wooden struts, which slant outwards from the temple building to brace the roof. In contrast, the Far Eastern architect uses a more complicated system of horizontal and vertical brackets to solve the weight problem. Although various dynasties ruled the valley successively in the past, the basic temple form was carried on without any changes except for the perfection of the outer embellishments and technology. Plan form continued with the pure and simple Vedic tradition which proved that the form of Nepalese temple was guided by religious concepts.

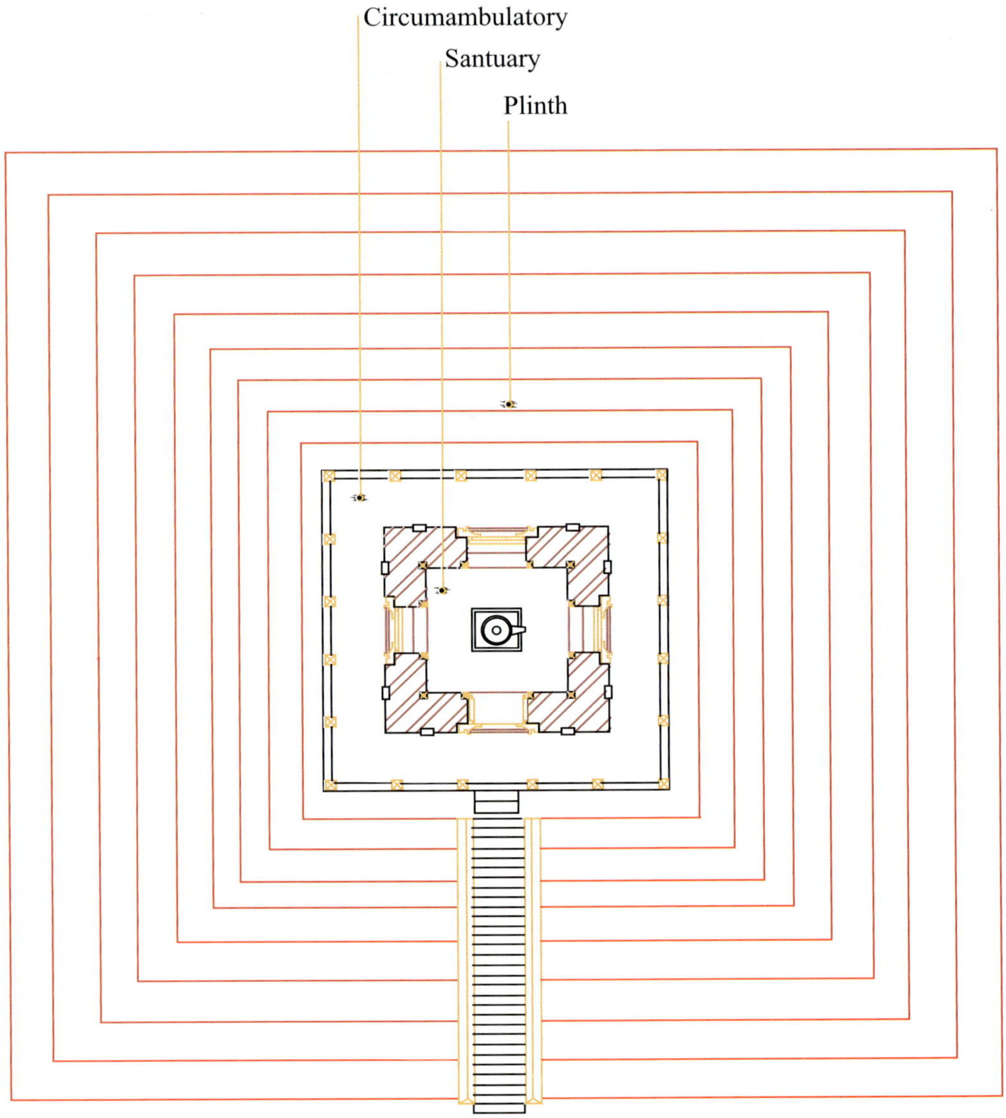

Figure 1. *Plan of Maju Dega At Durbar Square Kathmandu (w. Korn)*

In a few but prominent cases, the tiered temple plan is square in shape, in rare cases octagonal, circular and rectangular shapes are also found. Temples of rectangular shape in plan are generally dedicated to Bhairab, Bhimsen, Balkumari and other tantric gods and goddesses. The doors used to enter these temples are located on the longer side and the shorter side has symmetrically placed windows. These temples have an upper sanctum room with the image of the cult on the ground floor for general worshipping.

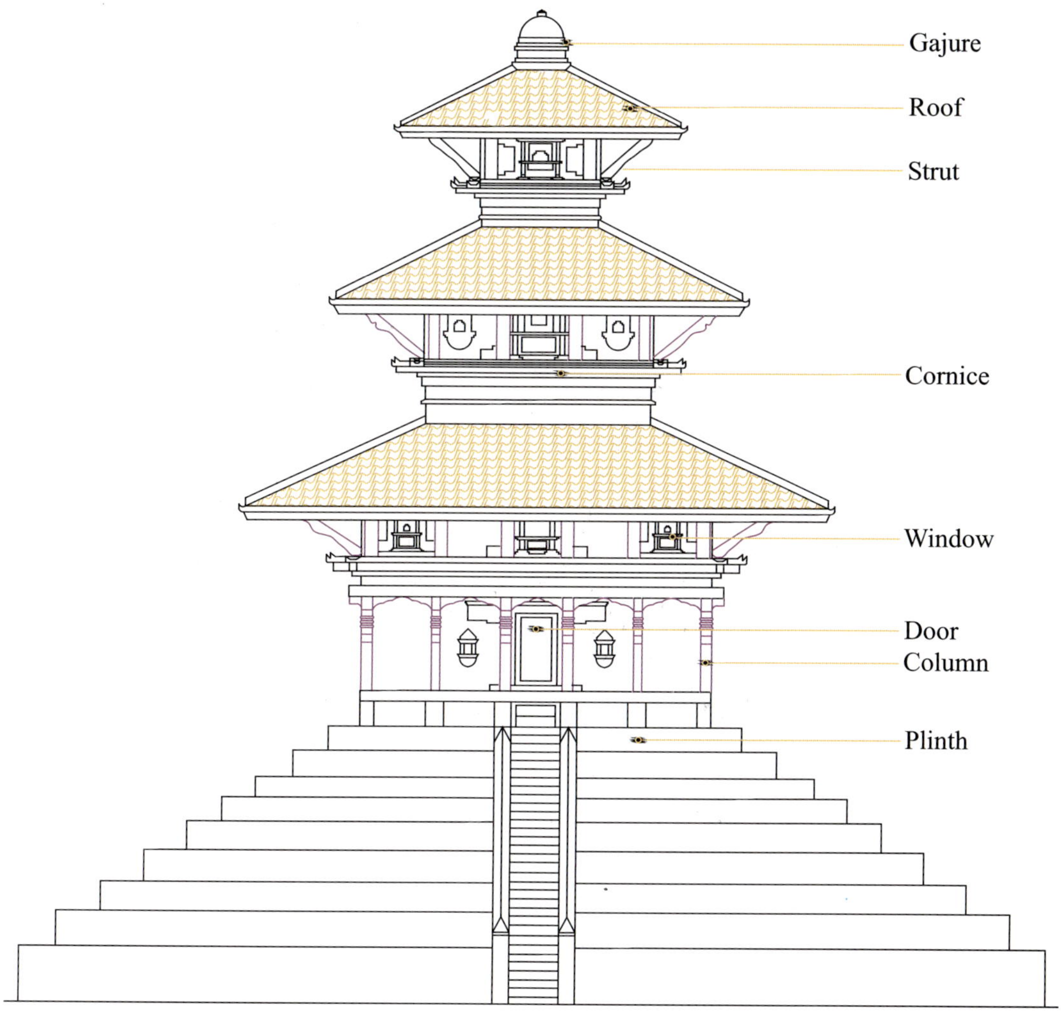

Figure 2. *Elevation of Maju Dega At Durbar Square Kathmandu (w. Korn)*

Religious Distinctions

The intermingling of Hindu and Buddhist deities and rituals is a remarkable and rich phenomenon in Nepal. The temple is similarly non-denominational and houses Hindu or Buddhist icons.

In Kathmandu valley one can distinguish between two fundamental types of shrines in temple structures, those revealing 'genius loci', i.e. those housing a deity 'found' at a site, and those housing an 'installed' deity. These differences have several implications for the conception of the temple. Those of the genius loci variety are never raised on plinths as the god emerges from the earth, and ground floors are conceived as open arcades instead of masonry walls.

Installed deities, especially those of royal donations, incorporate the stepping plinth as an eloquent counterpoint to the stepping form of the roofs above. The latter is typified by royal donations, often in prominent urban sites.

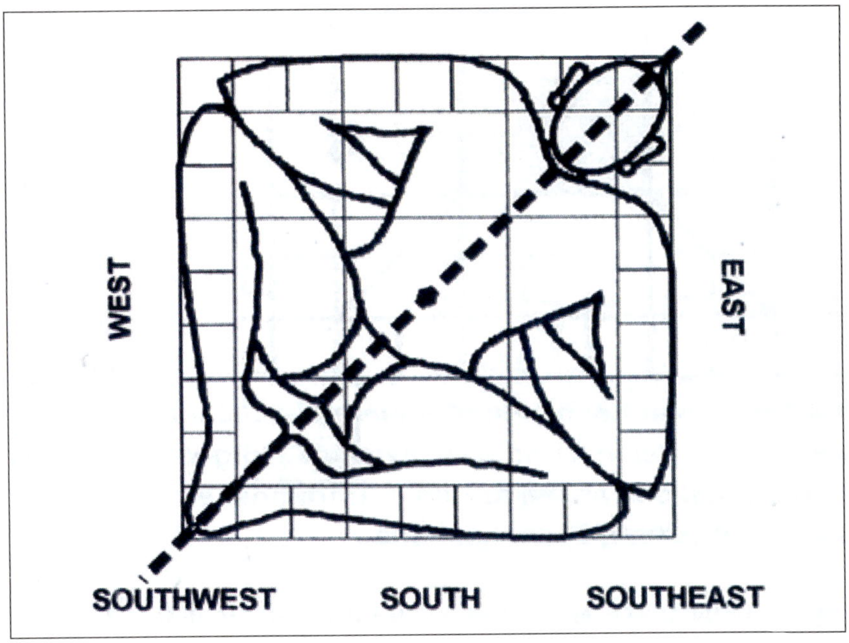

Plate I A. *Vastupurusha Mandala*

The most common temple plan of square shape is based on Vastupurusa mandala[2]. This mandala according to Hindus, is a map of the universe and also a geometric projection of the world, brought further into focus. The three-dimensional structure arises from the two dimensional plan with the mandala as blueprint. The mandala of the temple plan is also considered a symbolic pantheon of the gods. The large square of the Vastupurusha mandala is divided into eighty-one smaller squares. The smaller squares of the mandala are each the seat of a particular deity. The central ninth square is usually occupied by Brahma or some other prominent deity concerned with creation. Around the central ninth square various deities like the sun and moon, the dikpalas or guardians of the directions and various planetary divinities are arranged. From this cosmic ground plan the temple arises.

Several variations that are found within this square form are:

- Temple with square sanctum room and single doorway on the main side. The image of the god Narayana stands against the rear wall.
- Temple with square sanctum room and four doorways in cardinal points. The image of the god usually Shiva is centrally located.
- Temple with square form having three sides open. The idol of the god to whom the temple is dedicated, usually Ganesh or gods and goddesses worshipped with sacrifice of animals, is placed against the rear wall.
- Temple with a square sanctum room formed by inner core wall enclosed by an outer core wall forming inner circumambulatory path. The outer core walls have wide doorways each on four sides. The deity which is generally Shiva and occasionally Narayan is centrally placed. In some temple exterior wall is replaced by a colonnade as shown in figure 1 of Maju Temple[3] of Kathmandu.

In this type of temples the inner space of the ground floor is usually meant for the sanctuary and does not have internal floors in the upper levels nor are there any stairways to reach the upper levels. These upper levels remain empty. Hatches in the ceiling of the sanctuary are provided to allow access for repairs.

The gilt pinnacle or Gajura on top, representing the essence of the celestial world, crowns the composition like an antenna to spread and receive 'the word'. A gilt metal pinnacle is placed on top of the roof and this pinnacle is sometimes crowned by an umbrella.

The roofs of the temples are covered with clay tiles. Only in some cases, temples have either the top roof or all roofs covered with metal, generally copper. The design and details of the roof construction are basically the same in all temples. Sometimes the diminishing tiers above are reflected in a stepping plinth below, which raises the sanctuary many meters above the ground level.

The struts with many types of sculptural details support the massive roof overhanging of the temple. The joint where they meet are finished by the eaves board (horizontal member) in one line.

Wall openings reflect iconographic and symbolic aspirations more than the need to ventilate or light the interior space; most openings are very tiny in relation to the decorative and sculptural frames.

In the simplest two-tiered scheme, the walls of an inner shrine extend up through the lower roof to carry the upper roof, with the lower roof carried by an additional outer wall. In some temples a continuous ambulatory is created by providing a timber arcade.

Most of the temples stand on multiple receding plinths. Smaller temples stand only on one plinth. On the topmost plinth is erected the temple which is reached by a flight of steps attached to the plinths.

Plate I. *B Maju Temple View from North East, Kathmandu*

Notes

1. Pashupatinath temple is regarded as the most sacred temple of Lord Shiva. Pashupatinath dates back to 400 A.D and houses the linga, symbols of Shiva. Located on the banks of the sacred Bagmati River, the temple has a two-tiered gold plated roof and richly carved silver doors.
2. Vastupurusha mandala is one such mandala which forms an integral part of vastu shastra- the ancient Hindu canons of architecture and town planning.
3. Maju Temple is a three tiered temple with the dimension of 8.44m x 8.40 m. in ground floor. This temple is dedicated to Shiva and is located in Kathmandu Durbar Square. It was constructed in 1690 A.D. by Riddhi Laxmi , the widow of Parthivendra Malla.

Chapter 2

Traditional Construction Techniques

The traditional construction of temple (mandir) employs load bearing brick walls laid in yellow clay mortar (Newari-mhâsuchâ) together with a secondary timber frame .The timber frame construction like wall plates, corner posts and rafters are connected by timber pegs and lap joint.

In temple construction many types of the bricks were used depending upon its position. Bricks have been used not only as structural material but also for decorative purposes. Wall thickness varies considerably depending upon the number of storeys. The structural wall construction consists of three layers of brick with few cross bonds. These structural walls have sun-dried bricks in the inner part, wedge-shaped bricks called Dachi apã on the outer surface and brick fragment in the middle. To protect clay mortar being washed away by rain, minimum brick joints are provide by using Dachi apã. Besides its wedge shape, it is less porous and has a smooth surface to make it durable and prevent deterioration. Laid tightly, the lustrous brown crimson dachi apã provides a fine and smooth background for the sculptural effects of the woodcarving. Historically the walls are built of mud mortar and pointed with a traditional resin mixture of surkhi, lime, molasses, and ghee (Newari-silậy). The preparation of silậy (a lost art) is complicated and expensive. In general the construction of masonry walls in the last century has only employed yellow clay for mortar. This clay is from rubble and plant materials and is relatively strong and resilient mortar material.

Specially moulded bricks are used for decorative windows and cornice supporting the lower end of the slanting roof struts.

The most common fire bricks used in temples are:
Mã-apã- traditional brick with one end and one edge glazed
Bã-apã- moulded and decorated brick
Ku-apã-corner brick
Dachi-apã- it is both wedged and glazed.

Bepã-apã- stretcher
Tvah-apã-closer.

Different types of Bã-apã are used in various positions in temples. These positions are mostly cornice, lintel and plinth. Cornice layers have the following decorative Bã-apã in descending order:

- **Kahsimvaha-apã-** projecting brick with flower design generally with lotus leaf pattern

- **Mvah-apã-** brick with slanting and throating edge
- **Phecu apã-** brick with slanting edge (serves to repel pelting rain from the wall surface)

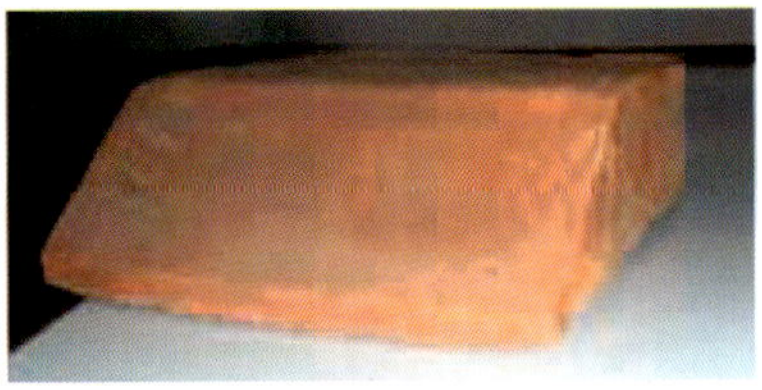

- **Palehah-apã-** lotus leaf

- **Dhalimvah-apã-** brick with stylized beam ends with the following patterns: skeleton face, lion face and flower

- **ãsa-apã-** brick with egg pattern (lowermost part of the cornice)

- **Jhallar-apã-** brick with frill design

- **Lhãhapã-** curved moulded bricks to support the lower end of the slanting roof struts. Four corners of temple at the cornice level of each storey usually have two layers of this bricks. These moulded bricks rest on top of a hand-shaped wooden piece called Lhãhphvah. These bricks are of the biggest size among other moulded bricks and become an important decorative element in the temple.
- **Mikhaphusi apã-** bricks used in lintels of decorative door and window.

- **Nãhgvahapã-** brick with snake patter

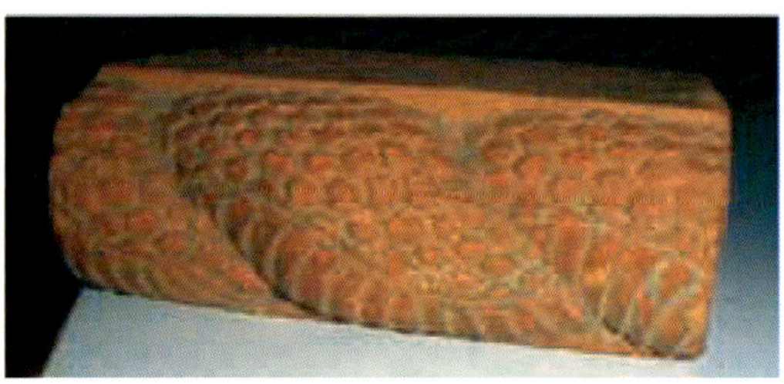

Plate II A. *View of Temple with Different Types of Bã-apã- (Moulded and Decorated Brick)*

The foundation structure of the temple is yet unknown because it has not been excavated. Stepped Plinth of temple not only serves as protection against damp and flooding, but more importantly as the aggrandizement of temple. Nyatapol temple[1] in Bhadgaun is set on a very high-stepped plinth structure of five levels and Taleju temple[2] in Kathmandu is set on twelve shallow plinths. The outer brick walls of plinth are faced with dachi apã and stone aprons.

The timber is used to maximum extent as structural material in temple for the construction of pillars, beams, brackets, struts, openings (door and windows), roofing purpose, etc. It is the intricate wood work that gives Nepalese architecture its unique appearance. Sal timber (shorea robusta) a local teak is traditionally employed for most structural and virtually all decorative timbers.

A temple with a circumbulatory has a wall on the inner side and isolated columns on the outer side. These outer columns are in a single row or double row depending upon the size of the temple. These columns support the upper brick work of the temple. These wooden columns are never replaced by stone or brick column in traditional temple structure.

Usually wooden columns are supported by a dressed natural stone (Ilohan) or a wooden threshold. The dado in stone are placed vertically along each column. The wooden column supports a wooden bracket which transfers the load from the lintel and beam on the column. Square shape of peg extending from the centre of the column, passes through the bracket into the beam and holds the three structural elements in position. The columns are joined to the beams Plate II B. Rafters in Lower Roof of Jaganath Temple View from West, Kathmandu by means of thick wooden studs at their upper extremity. The architrave is made of single length beam normally extending beyond the angle column. In such a case, the sub-beams placed at this spot are less extended, and the extremities of such parts are generally sculpted in the form of dragon heads. To the right of the angle columns, the sub beams and the brackets are joined by means of a halved joint notch assemblage.

Plate II B. *Rafters in Lower Roof of Jaganath Temple View from West, Kathmandu*

The framework of the different peripheral roofs at every floor of the temple consists of radiating rafters which are tied together by walls plates at the top and a horizontal beam at the bottom which is again supported by inclined struts. The traditional connection between rafter and wall plate and between rafter and horizontal beam consists of two timber pegs inserted to brace rafter against the horizontal member. The traditional method uses the timber peg to keep the various components of roof in place. Thus any damage to the timber peg may lead to the collapse of the roof as there is nothing to prevent the heavy rafters from sliding off the masonry core structure.

Diagonal struts have a mouth shape cut at the head to support the wall plate and level cut at the base to rest on the coping of the cornice. The wooden brackets supporting the ridge piece go right through the wall and the two extremities are fixed with wedges which exert pressure on both sides of the wall. The ridge piece is pegged on the brackets and in turn, the rafters are pegged on to the ridge piece and wall plate. Rafters placed at right angles to the eaves of the roof, stop near the top of the hip whereas the others spread out somewhat like a fan.

Most of the roofs of the temples are covered with special tiles called *Aenpậ*. Horizontal wooden planks are placed over rafters on top of which is laid 4cm to 10cm thick clay into which *Aenpậ*s are pressed. Special tiles are used for ridges and valleys called Kopus and Dokus respectively. In temples, rafters of the top most roof meet at a point on a central post, which is again covered with pinnacle (Gajure) made of burnt clay or gilded sheet copper.

Plate II C. *View of Roof Tile (Aenpậs)*

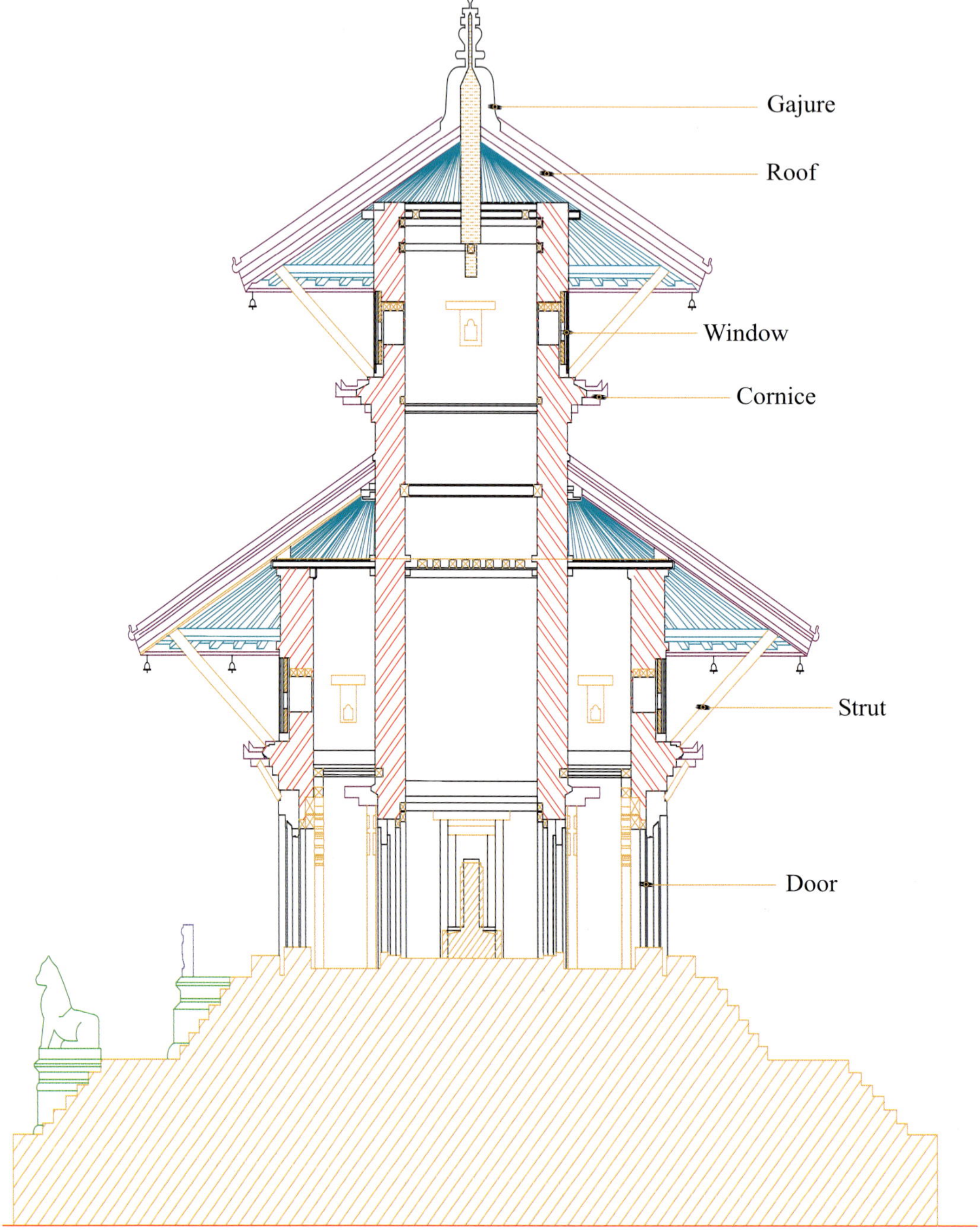

Figure 3. *Section of Char Narayan Dega at Durbar Square Patan (W. Korn)*

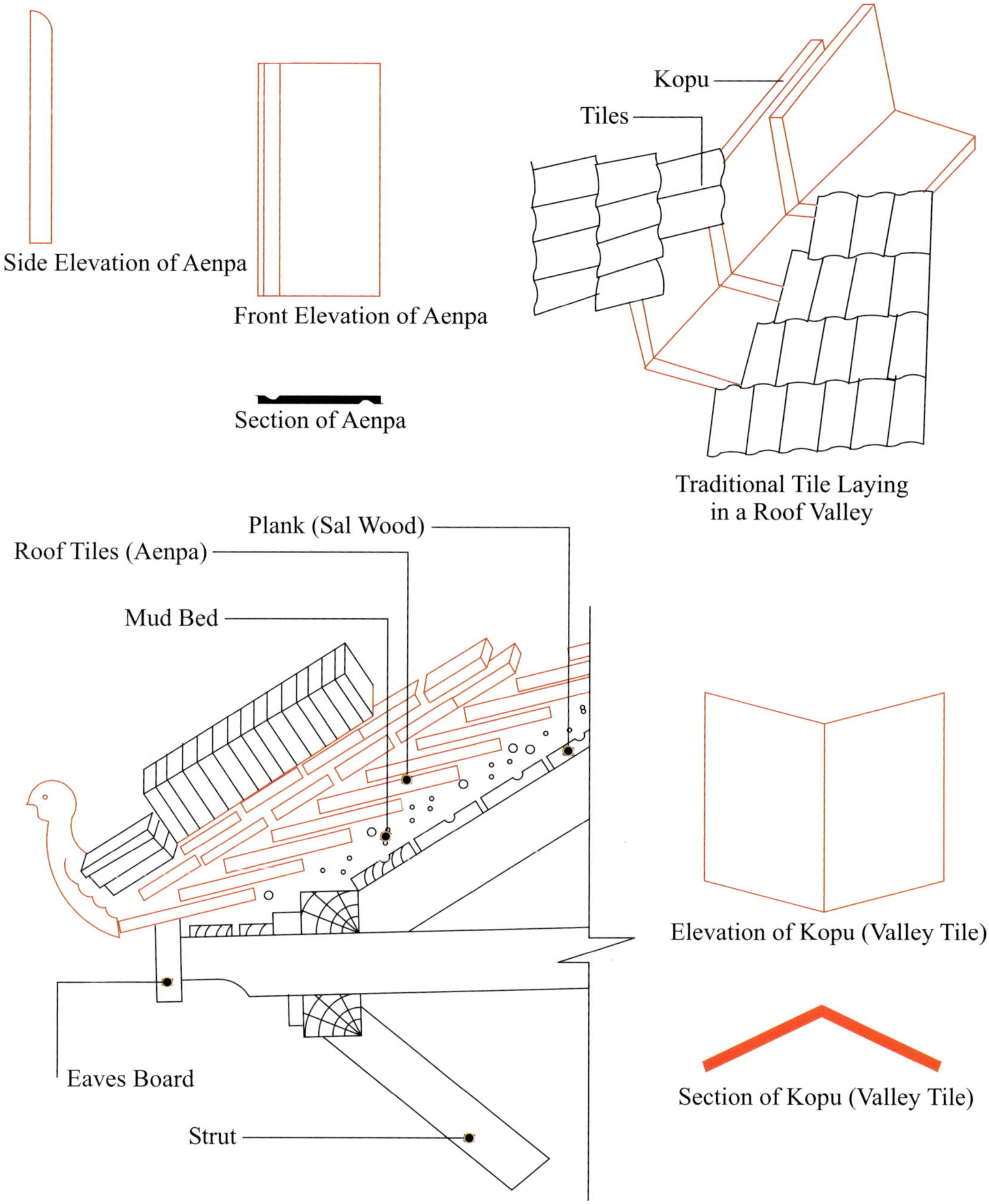

Figure 4. *Section of Traditional Tile Laying on a Hip Rafter (G. Toffin)*

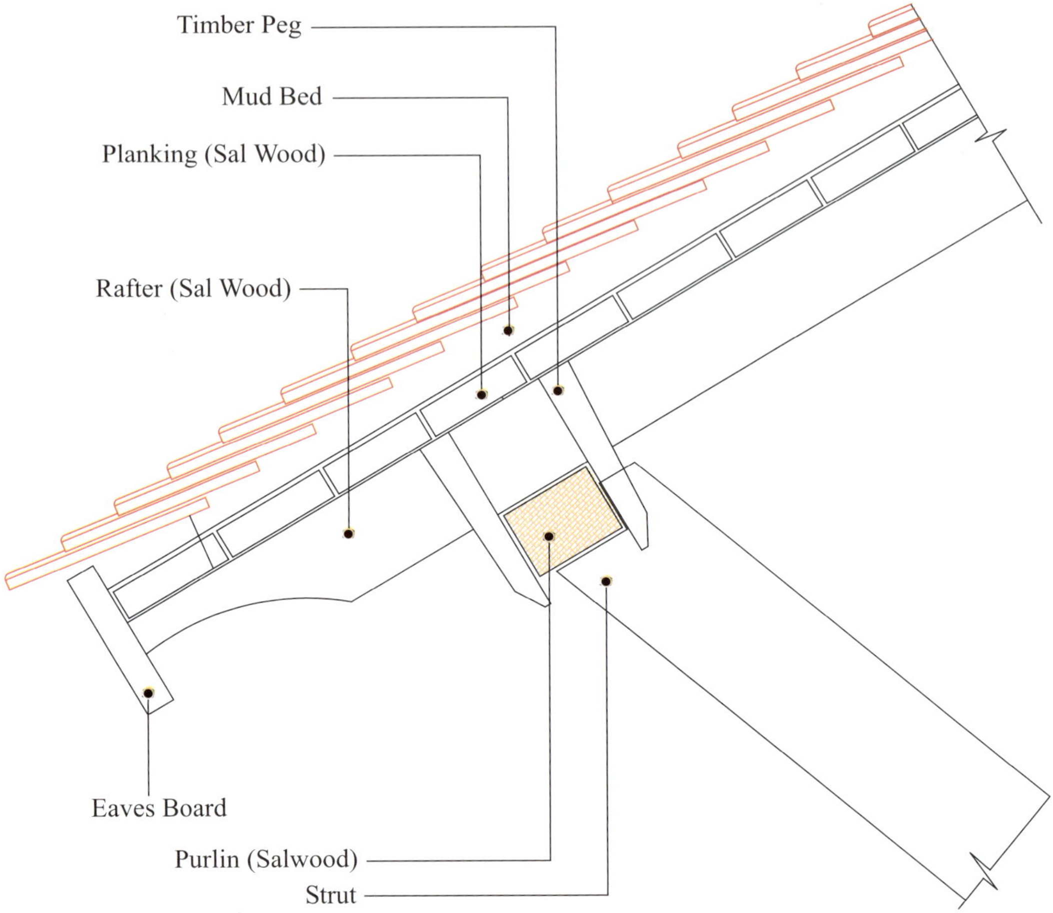

Figure 5. *Section at Roof Overhang (Traditional Method)*

Proportion

The Hindu precepts relating to the proportion of plan and elevation in temples can be found in many ancient scriptures. The design module (ya) of the temple determined in "The protection of temple" (deveraya raksana) are 6 for two-storied pagoda, 9 for a three-storied and 15 for a five storied one. The design module of nine for a three storied temple is marked at the base of the temple which is equal to the width of the temple. The reduction in size of the successive width of each storey is determined by reducing the width by three modules. The design module of nine will have the width of six modules in the first storey and three modules in the top storey. The design module of three remains the same whether it is two storeys or five storeys as shown in Manuscript of Nyatapola temple of Bhakatapur. Grid division of 15 parts is taken for five tired temple.

In determining the ideal height of a temple, the Nepali builders appear to have followed the Matsyapurana which prescribes that the total height of the temple should be twice or three times the width of the temple plan. For nine modules the height of temple should be eighteen modules. This is true with temples facing the east direction e.g. temple of the Char Narayan Temple[3] of Patan (Refer figure 6.and plate II E).

According to the old manuscript the elevation of a temple could be conceived as a Yantra. This is the technical term for the geometrical pattern so often used to give a tangible shape to ideas about deities. The three storied temple of Kankaswore[4] on the banks of Bishnumati river is embedded into Yantra (Refer Plate II C) consists of two components: (i) the well-known hexagon which is formed by two interlocking triangles and (ii) a rhomboid made up of two equilateral triangles showing the common baseline. These two triangles according to Hindu emblems are symbols of male for a triangle pointing upward and female for a triangle pointing downward. In joining them, the hexagon shows the male and female in conjunction, i.e. in the process of creation.

An old manuscript of Kankeswore also shows the use of three proportioning triangles to determine the heights of important elements in elevation, e.g. eaves level of roofs, cornice level with lion faces, junction level of lower roofs and upper core walls. Three elements mentioned in the manuscript are: i) the ornamental layer ii) proportion of slope iii) the height of brick work. The thickness of the wall has been one of the primary concerns of Vastushastra since it directs the overall proportion. One of the key components of proportionate planning is the wall of the temple. The thickness of the wall of Kankeswore temple is half the width of the sanctum .The actual measurement of Kankeswore temple at present tally with the measurement obtained from the manuscript.

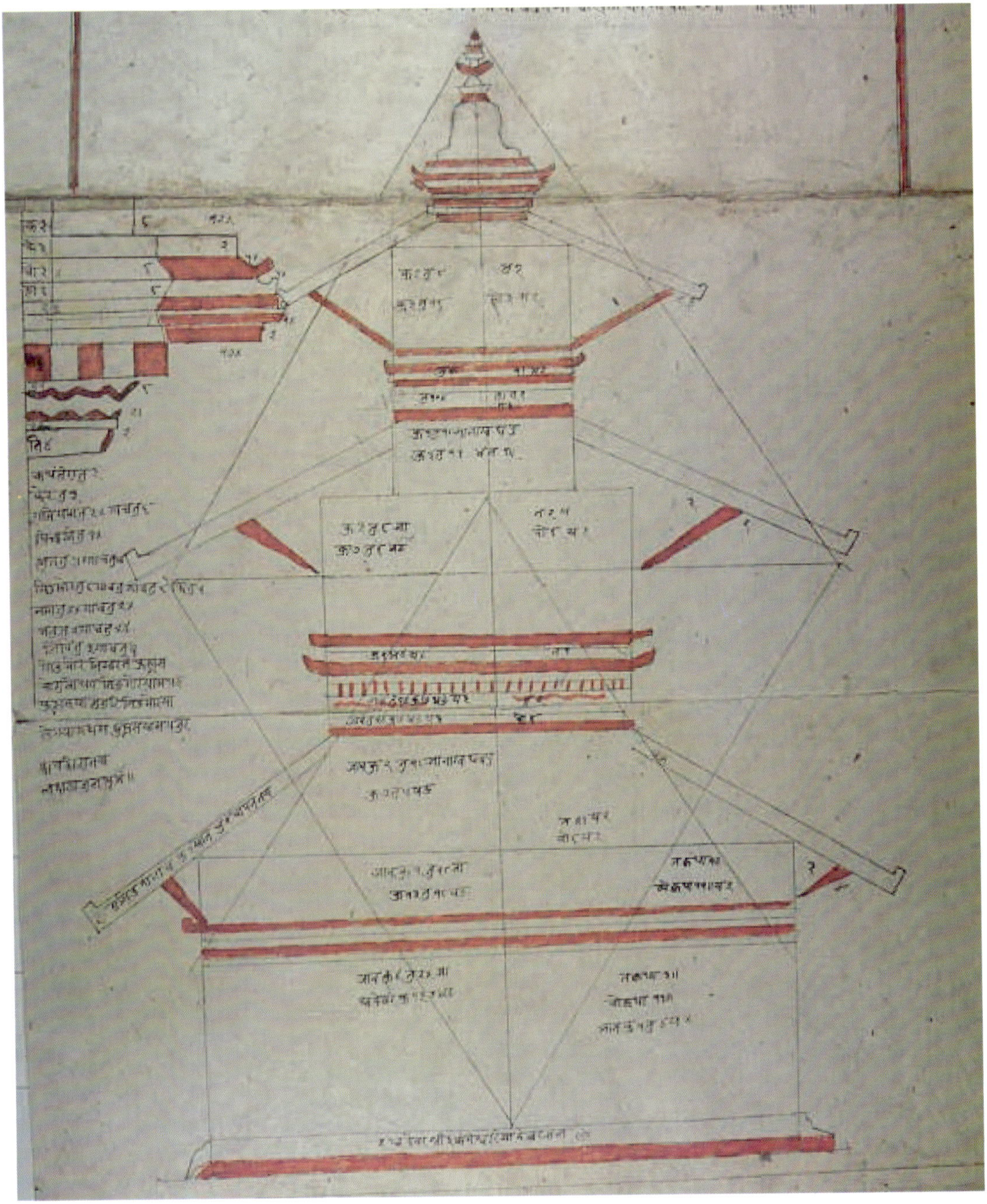

Plate II D. *Manuscript of Kankeswore Temple , Kathmandu*

PlateII E. *Kankeswore Temple View from South, Kathmandu*

(i) The ornamental layer consists of seven horizontal sections. The first three is the floor of the upper storey (the clay part and the beam). Then there are three courses of straight bricks without ornamentation. The intermediate layer consists of a string of bricks with a rounded profile slightly protruding from the straight vertical line of wall called nahgvah. The last layer of cornice is of Sim Mara, i.e. the lion faces protruding from the vertical line.

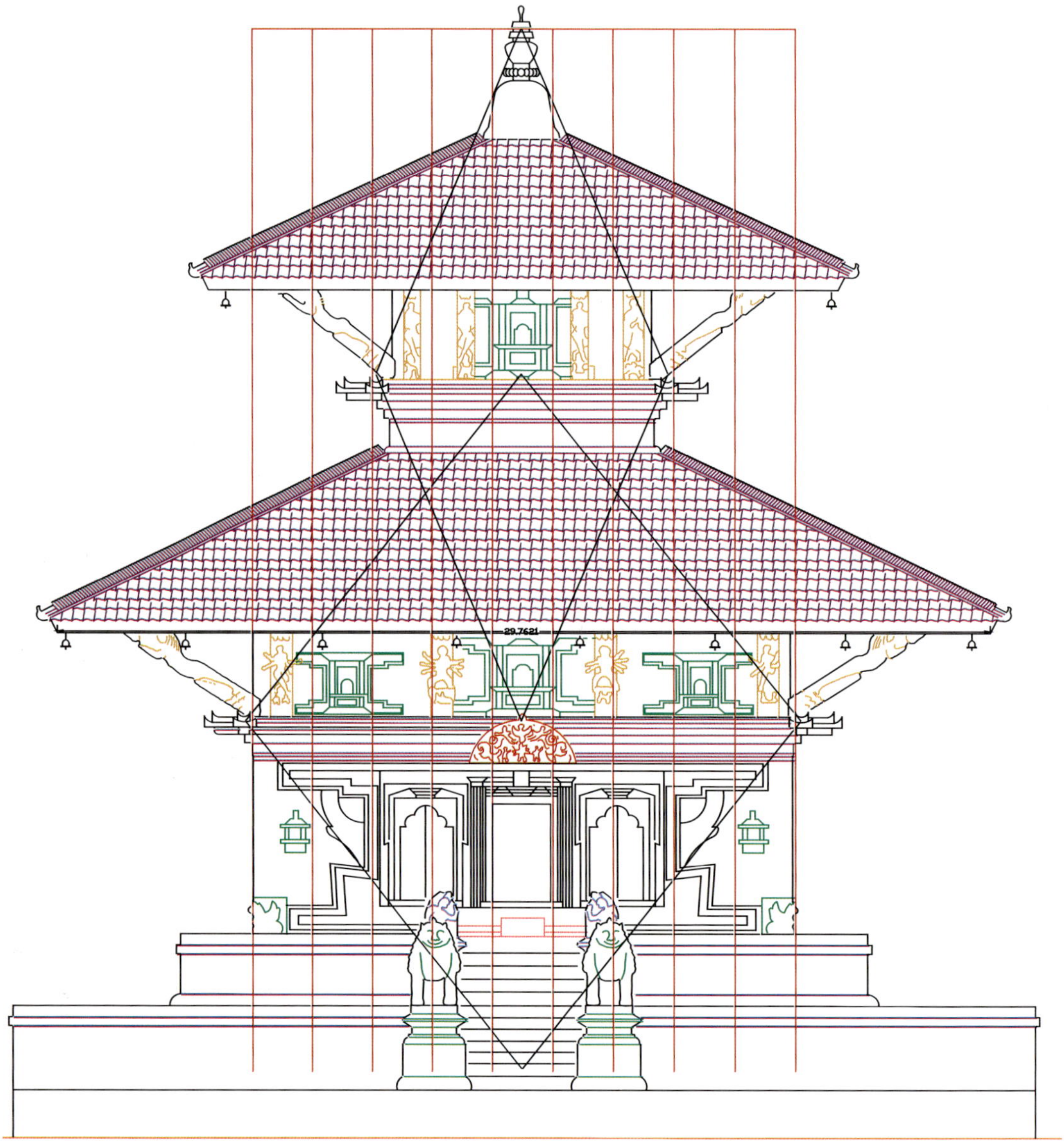

Figure 6. *Proportion of Char Narayan Dega at Durbar Square Patan*

(ii) The instruction concerning roofs is very short. Slope of roof struts are given as the inside x part and outside y part. The outside part is the one which protrudes outward from the point where struts meet beam, inside part lies between this joint and the brickwork. The proportion of slope is mentioned as 2:1 and 3:2.

(iii) The dimension of brickwork is mentioned in each storey and is different from storey to storey. These are defined by side length (jhara) and height (Jao) which are given in unit or module.

Plate II F. *Charnarayan Temple View from East. Patan*

Manuscript has shown that every part of the temple is rigorously controlled by a proportional system of measurement and interrelated by the use of fundamental unit. Only if the temple is constructed according to a mathematical system can it be expected to function in harmony with the mathematical basis of the universe.

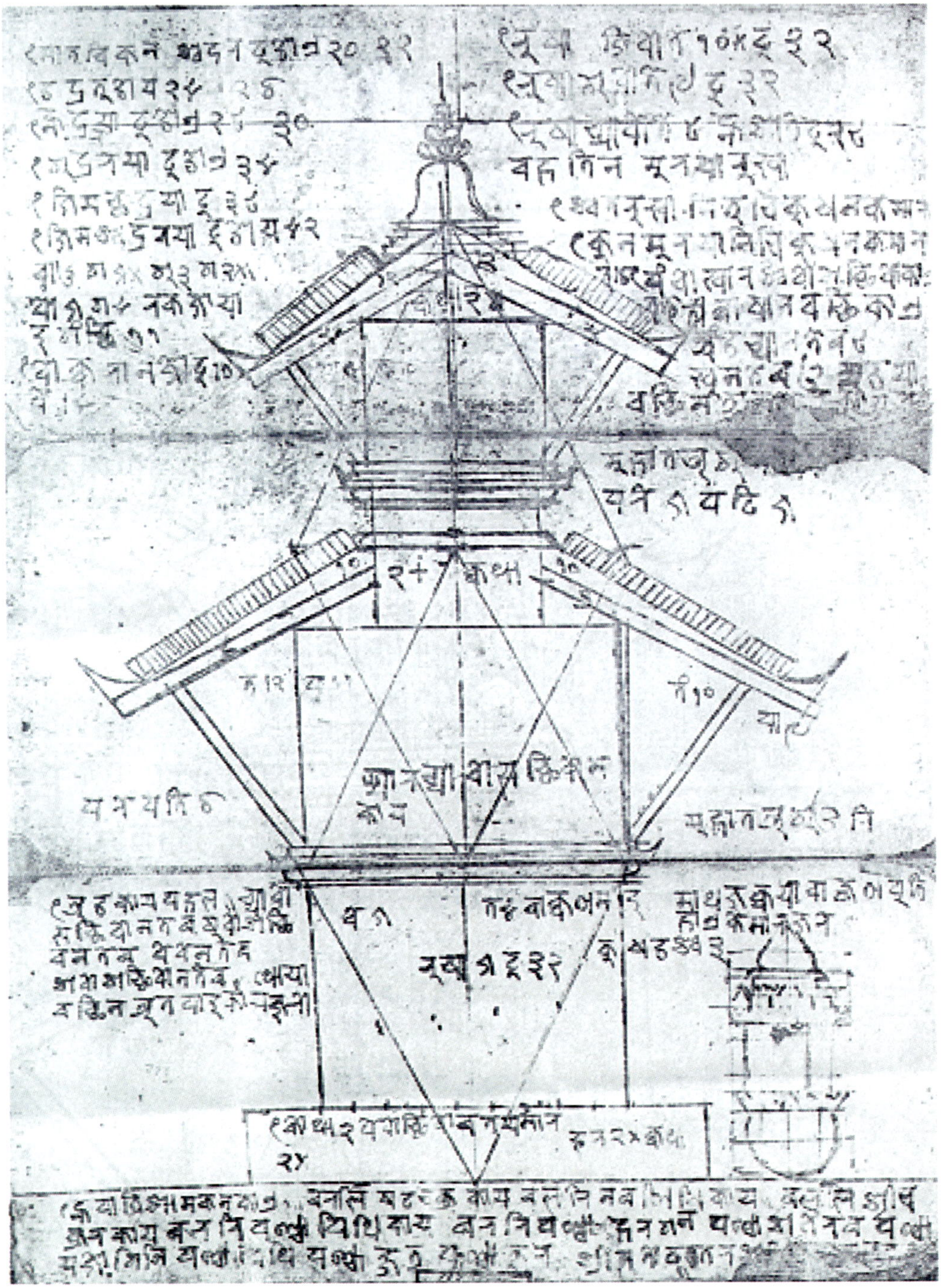

Plate II G. *Manuscript of Char Narayan Temple Showing Proportion*

Measurement in the Hindu temple is not confined to architecture. The sacred images of the temple, whether carved or painted, are also subject to strict mathematical control in the discipline of iconometry. Only a well-executed image, satisfactory in its proportional measurements will be able to invite the deity to reside within it. Thus the welfare of the community and the happiness of its members, depend upon the correctly proportioned temple. Architectural texts stress that only work that is completed according to the rules will gain the desired merit for its builder.

The Shukranatisara, an iconographical text, states that "the image not made with the prescribed rules is fruitless and its worship is without any effect". Various canons of proportions are found in the texts on image making which mostly proposes the face length, i.e. distance from the top of the forehead to the bottom of the chin as the module (Tala) for the figure. Each Tala is further divided into twelve amgulas.

The instruction of proportion and orientation mentioned in manuscript is not self-evident. It allows us to form at least some idea of the processes the Newar architects used in their design.

Unit of Measurement

The basic unit of measurement in Kathmandu valley during the Malla period was the cubit Ku. (The distance from elbow to the top of middle finger which is equal to 45.72cm.or 18"). It consists of 24 fingers (amgule "am" or thumbs "tu"). One thumb or "tu" is equal to 1.9 cm. Other unit of measurement includes the span of an outstretched hand from the thumb to the tip of the little finger called Kurate or Kola. This is equal to 22.86 cm or 9".A small stroke slanting upward called yo (') a quarter is used as a subdivision of "tu" and "ku" up to three strokes.

Orientation

In the manuscript (devaraya raksana) transcribed by Kolver (1996), orientation of the temple is fixed by dividing side length of temple by eight. The side length of the temple is expressed in amgule before dividing by eight. The remainder of this division determines the direction, each of the digits from zero to seven being assigned to one of the cardinal direction beginning in the north east which has value of zero (rikta). Other succession directions are 1 for east (flag), 2 for south east (Crow), 3 for south (lion), 4 for southwest (dog), 5 for west (bull), 6 for North West (monkey), 7 for north (elephant). Every single direction has its specific meaning. The meanings of different directions indicated by followings figures are: flag (1) constant feeling of good fortune, the crow (2) constant feeling of anxiety, the lion (3) constant feeling of the state of conquered enemies, dog (4) constant feeling of infirmity, bull (5) constant feeling of certain sorrow, monkey (6) constant feeling of fickleness of women, elephant (7) constant feeling of tranquility/happiness. Predictably, one sees the even numbers are inauspicious, which means intermediate directions ought to be avoided. Flag (1), Lion (3) and Elephant (7) are the auspicious orientation for deciding the frontal direction of temple.

Notes

1. Nyatapol temple is a five tiered temple located in Taumadi tole near durbar square of Bhaktapur. The temple is dedicated to tantric goddess Siddhi Laxmi. This temple was constructed in 1702 A.D by Bhupatindra Malla (The most impressive work is on the 108 struts illustrating the diverse forms of Bhagawati mahishamardini). The base of the temple measure 9m. x.9m. and height of 22.5 m. to the top of its pinnacles from it plinth.
2. Taleju temple was built in 1576 A.D. by Mahendra Malla is situated in Hanuman Dhoka of Kathmandu Durbar Square. The temple is over 37m high resting on a twelve stage plinth. This temple has taleju Bhavani or Durga and patron goddess of Malla King.
3. Char Narayan temple was built in1566 A.D. by king Purandaerasinha and is situated in Patan Durbar Square. It is 6.62 m x 6.63 m in plan and is of two tiers. It is dedicated to the god Narayan.
4. Kankeswore temple is situated next to Bishnumati river and is a two tiered temple. This temple is dedicated to chamunda, one of eight matrikas, but there are no icons within shrine. Only plain stones which, shows tantric origin. This temple was constructed in 1644 A.D.

Chapter 3

Pinnacle (Gajura)

The Pinnacle (Gajura) is the topmost part of the temple. It is symbolically the most significant part in the temple. The size and shape of the temple, as well as the deity to which the temple is dedicated, determines the style of the pinnacle. Generally square plan temples have a single pinnacle and rectangular plan temples have more than one pinnacle. Only a few temples with rectangular plan have more than one Gajura, e.g. Kashi Bishwonath Temple[1]of Bhaktapur (Plate III C), Bagh Bhairabh Temple[2] in Kirtipur. In a few large temples of rectangular plan pinnacle is also placed at the lower roof with their back joined to the brick wall behind them. Bagh Bhairabh Temple in Kirtipur has 18 pinnacles in total. The first roof has one pinnacle, the second roof has six, the third roof has ten and the top roof has one. A temple of square plan but with secondary deity on its plinth

Plate III A. *Pinnacle of Pachali Mahadev Temple, Kathmandu*

has more than one pinnacle. Changu Narayan temple[3] (Plate III F) and Taleju Temple[4] (Plate III G) of Kathmandu have five Gajura out of which four smaller sizes at each corner surround the large pinnacle at the centre.

The pinnacle is placed over the timber post (Galahtha) supported by the horizontal beam (Galahsi) fixed to the brick wall. The base of the pinnacle usually consists of multiple flat layers of varying height which end in upturned corners. The shape of these sculptural bases is reminiscent of the abstract form of cornice beams which extend at the corners of most temples below the strut level. Above this base is an extremely flattened pair of circular

Figure 7. *Elevation of Gajure (Y.R. Bajracharya)*

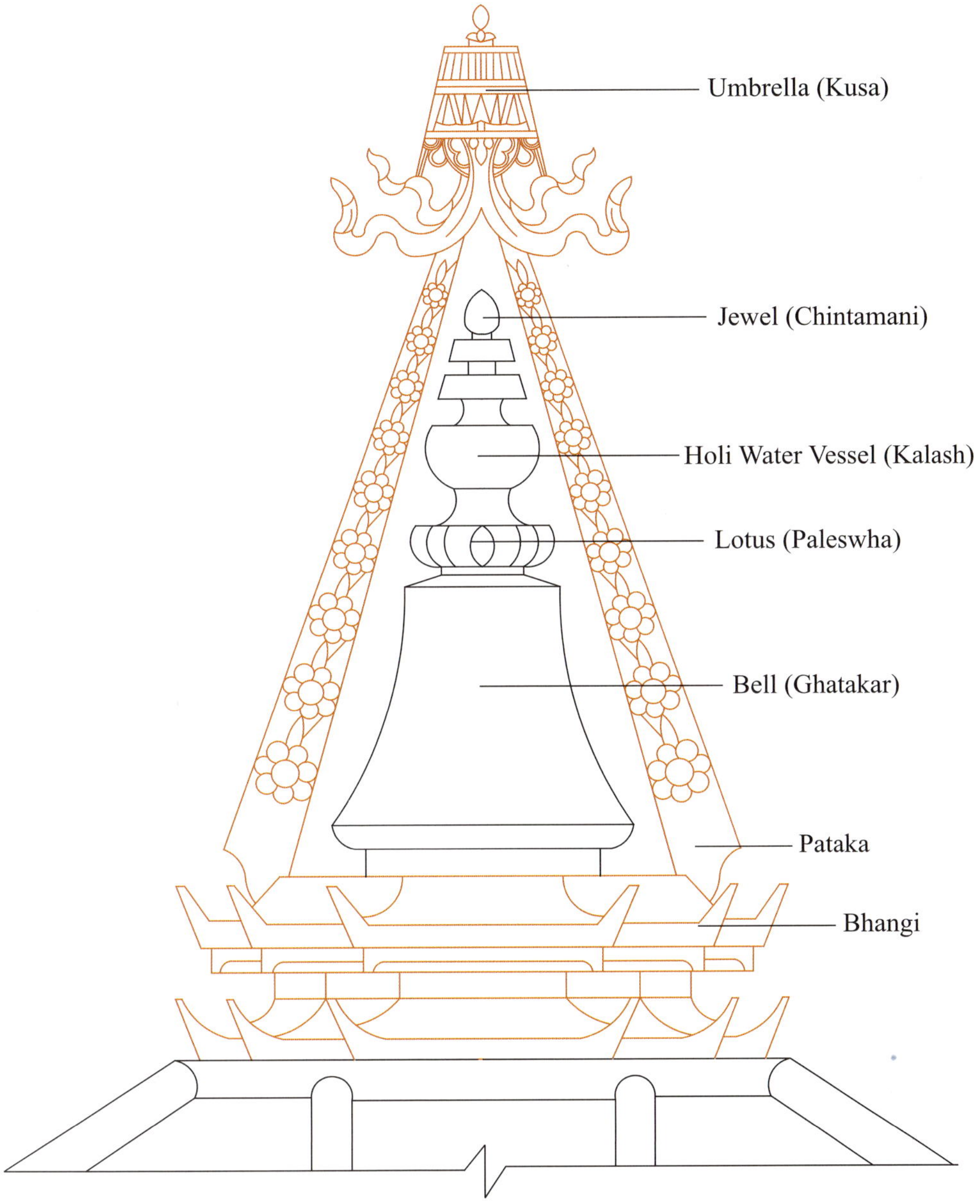

Figure 8. *Elevation of Gajure (Y.R. Bajaracharya)*

rings which are basic to all pinnacles as shown in Plate III A of Pachali Mahadev Temple[5], Kathmandu. In general, a pinnacle usually has four parts (i) Jewel (ii) Kalash (iii) Lotus (iv) bell.

(i) Jewel is a final or pointed culmination of the pinnacle which represents a sacred jewel. This Jewel rests on a series of three tiny rings.

(ii) Kalash is a sphere representing the holy water pot considered as the most appropriate symbol of creative element and of life itself.

(iii) Lotus is a small spherical division divided into petal-like segments as a symbolic lotus design. It acts as a base to the Kalash.

(iv) Bell occupies the largest portion of a pinnacle and it is the lowest portion of the pinnacle. It rests on a border of circular forms which serve as decorative edging for the flattened bell-shaped pinnacle. The overall shape of a pinnacle is more or less the shape of a bell. The bell is considered the symbol of vibration and the cosmic creative force. It plays an important part in Hindu as well as Buddhist rituals.

Plate III B. *Detail View of Pinnacle, Pachali Mahadev Temple, Kathmandu*

Most Nepalese temples have a sacred umbrella mounted over the pinnacle. This umbrella symbolizes protectionism from the religious point of view. There is no umbrella on top of plaster pinnacles. This protective umbrella of many layers goes back to pre-Buddhist times as a sacred object and continues in Nepal till date, as one of the eight most auspicious symbols. It is believed that all deity images should have a canopy or umbrella over them. As an indication of supreme veneration, the umbrella is mounted over the temple spire in honour of the holy precincts, but especially of the deity enshrined within them. This umbrella is always made of metal and brightly gilded, standing over a gilded pinnacle in most cases.

Plate III C. *Pinnacles of Kasi Bishwonath Temple, Bhaktapur*

As pinnacles vary in design, so do the umbrellas, ranging from two to thirteen stages in height. Each umbrella is mounted on a central support and is slightly smaller than the one below it.

The Shiva-Parvati temple[6] of Kathmandu, Darbar Square is crowned by a triple pinnacles with three small umbrellas mounted on a supportive frame of bronze (Plate III D). This frame is quite ornate, exemplifying only one of many that the frame in itself has any symbolic significance, but its role in supporting the honorific umbrella makes it an important device. This pinnacle of three spires has double bronze flags on rod supports at all four corners of the pinnacle base as an additional auspicious symbol, in honour of the temple goddess.

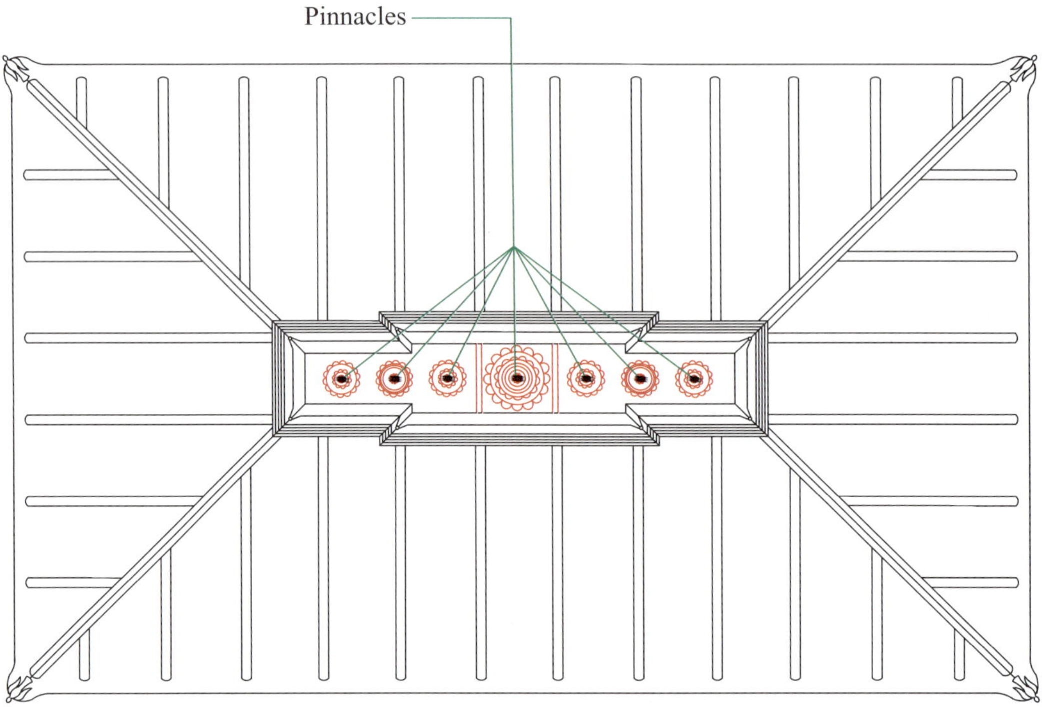

Figure 9. *Roof Plan of Kasi Bishwonath Temple, Bhaktapur*

Plate III D. *Pinnacles of Shiva Parvati Temple, Kathmandu*

The Maju temple[7] in Kathmandu Durbar Square is perhaps best known for the special pinnacle which has the base in the shape of a Buddhist stupa. This is the only example so far discovered of such a symbol of Buddhism on the pinnacle of a Shiva temple. The temple of Buddhist deity has a stupa at the base of Pinnacle like the temple of the Harati Mata[8] in Swayambhu.

The triple spire, for instance, is symbolic of Brahma, Vishnu, and Mahesvara on Hindu temples, and Buddha, Dharma, and Sangha are symbolized on Buddhist temples. The spire itself stands on a flat base attached to the top of the temple.

Plate III E. *Pinnacles of Changu Narayan Temple*

Note

1. Kashi Bishwonath Temple was built by Bhupatindra Mall in 1708 A.D. It is a three tiered temple situated in Taumadhi tole of Bhaktapur. Like other Bhairab temples, this temple is of rectangular plan.There are fifty six carved roof struts depicting the forms of Bhagbati and Matrika goddesses. The lower two roofs are tiled whilst the upper is gilded and crowned with a set of seven beautiful toranas.
2. Bagh Bhairabh Temple - This is a three-storey rectangular temple of Bagh Bhairab or Tiger God. The temple was built in 1671 A.D. It is located in Kirtipur and is devoted to the incarnation of Bhairab as a tiger.
3. Changu Narayan temple- is the oldest temple in the Kathmandu Valley, displaying some of the valley's finest examples of stone, wood, and metal craftsmanship of the Lichchhavi period (400-750 AD). The temple is devoted to Lord Narayan (another name for Vishnu) and is a two tiered temple, square in plan with dimension of 10m x10m in ground floor. It was built in 325 A.D. north of Bhaktapur at a distance of two miles on a hillock called Changu.
4. Pachali Mahadev Temple- is considered as one of the best examples of temple architecture from the Shah dynasty. Laxmeshwar Mahadev temple is cardinally arranged, square in plan and is designed upon two mitered stone platform. The enclosed square sanctum houses a sacred Shiva Lingam which is surrounded by a circumbulatory path formed by twenty carved wooden pillars; each pillar is seated on a stone carved winged lion. It is a three storied temple carved with clay tiles set in a clay bed. This temple was built in 1813 A.D. It is situated in Teku ward no. 12 of Kathmandu.
5. Shiva-Parvati temple- Shiva Parbati temple is situated in Durbar Square of Kathmandu opposite the famous Kumari Ghar. It is rectangular in shape and is of two storeys. It is built on a three step brick plateform, and its façade is almost completely taken by beautifully carved windows, doorways and toranas. There are two wooden figures one male shiva and one female parvati looking from open central window on the first floor. This temple was built in 1786-95 B.S. during the reign of king Rana Bahadur Shah.
6. Harati Mata temple -is a two tired temple with metal clad roof. It is situated to the north west of Swayambhu stupa. It was constructed in seventeenth century and is devoted to Hindu Goddess Harati Mata.

Chapter 4

Roof

In the temple, the roof is one of the elements which give it a unique appearance not only because of its general form and repeated sloping surfaces, but also because of individual ornamental and symbolic elements attached to it. The wood used for the basic skeleton of the roof complex comes from the Sal tree (*Shorea robusta*) supposed to be better than teak for building purposes. It is the hardest wood available in Nepal.

Each sloped roof has heavy rafters that fan out downwards from the core to meet the horizontal beam. This horizontal beam is supported by struts which slope upward from the cornice. The fanning rafters of the uppermost roof always extend to the centre of the core to form a peaked roof. Over the fanning rafters, flat wooden boards are placed horizontally on all four sides of the roof from the core to the lower roof edge. The boards are placed close together and are usually covered with a layer of mud or earth of 1 to 2 inches thickness. On top of the mud mortar fire-baked interlocking clay tiles are usually placed for all roofs whereas in some of the temples topmost roofs usually have metal plate roof. Clay tiles S-curve in section are always rectangular but vary in size from 5" to 8".The narrow ends of the tiles are notched to interlock with one another and they effectively pass rainwater down the roofs to their edges without letting any water seep in. The back edge of each tile hooks upward to catch the front edge of the tile behind it while the tile's front edge hooks under in turn to grip the end of the tile before it. At the hips and ridges of the roof angled tiles cover the joint of tiles at the meeting of two roof slopes, keeping rain from soaking into these important junctions. Nepalese temple roofs always have a raised edge along their sloping corners. This is to protect the corners from decaying at the joints of the wooden skeletal structure and to effectively keep water from seeping in. The best traditional method of protecting these sloping corners is with a covering of specially designed angular tiles which fit over the corner edge and join the flat tiles which cover the rest of the roof. Another traditional method of protecting the ridge of the slope roof is by placing small flat tiles standing on end along the entire length of the ridge to form a high protective rib.

A metal roof has a smooth surface with small ribs that follow the slope of the roof in parallel rows approximately two feet wide apart. These ribs are always in even numbers on each side of the roof. Ribs are mainly to join two metal plates with an overlapping joint between them. These small ribs have the attendant faces at the end. The attendant faces along their roof ribs are generally feminine in appearance and wear elaborate crowns of headdresses and are not fierce in expression. Another kind of head with mustachioed male is sometimes found at the end of corner rib. It is located slightly behind the upturned curves at the roof edge. These are placed to form the ends of the downward sloping ribs. The roof gilding is symbolic of purity, so genuine gold was used to cover the holiest of temples. But nowadays a mixture of copper, zinc and brass is usually used to make metal roof coverings.

For clay tile roofing, specially formed tiles with upward curve are placed at the overhanging corners of the temple roof. These corner tiles are called rupas, and seem to have no structural function, but they give the roof its graceful silhouette. The downward slope of the roof would be heavy and oppressive if the eye were directed only toward the ground, but the addition of these elements with their sprightly upward curve at the corners allows the viewer's eye to be re-directed upward and creates the illusion that the roofs are much lighter than they actually are.

For metal roofing, especially caste metal tiles are placed at the overhanging corners of a temple roof. Upward curve tiles of metal are usually part of a bronze bracket which is attached to the edge of the roof at the corner. These brackets are usually embossed with floral or geometric designs and it is integrated in its attachment to the edge of the roof.

The curves often have further additions, most notably birds. These small birds of metal are often perched upon the upward-curved tips of the corners. They sometimes adorn only the top roof of a multi-storey temple and sometimes are very numerous, adorning several roofs. The birds usually have their wings spread, as if ready to fly and they often hold leaf-shaped pendants of thin metal in their beaks. The general opinion is that they are basically decorative, but there is also some symbolic importance in the chirping of real birds as a kind of warning.

Plate IV A. *Roof of Bajrayogni Temple*

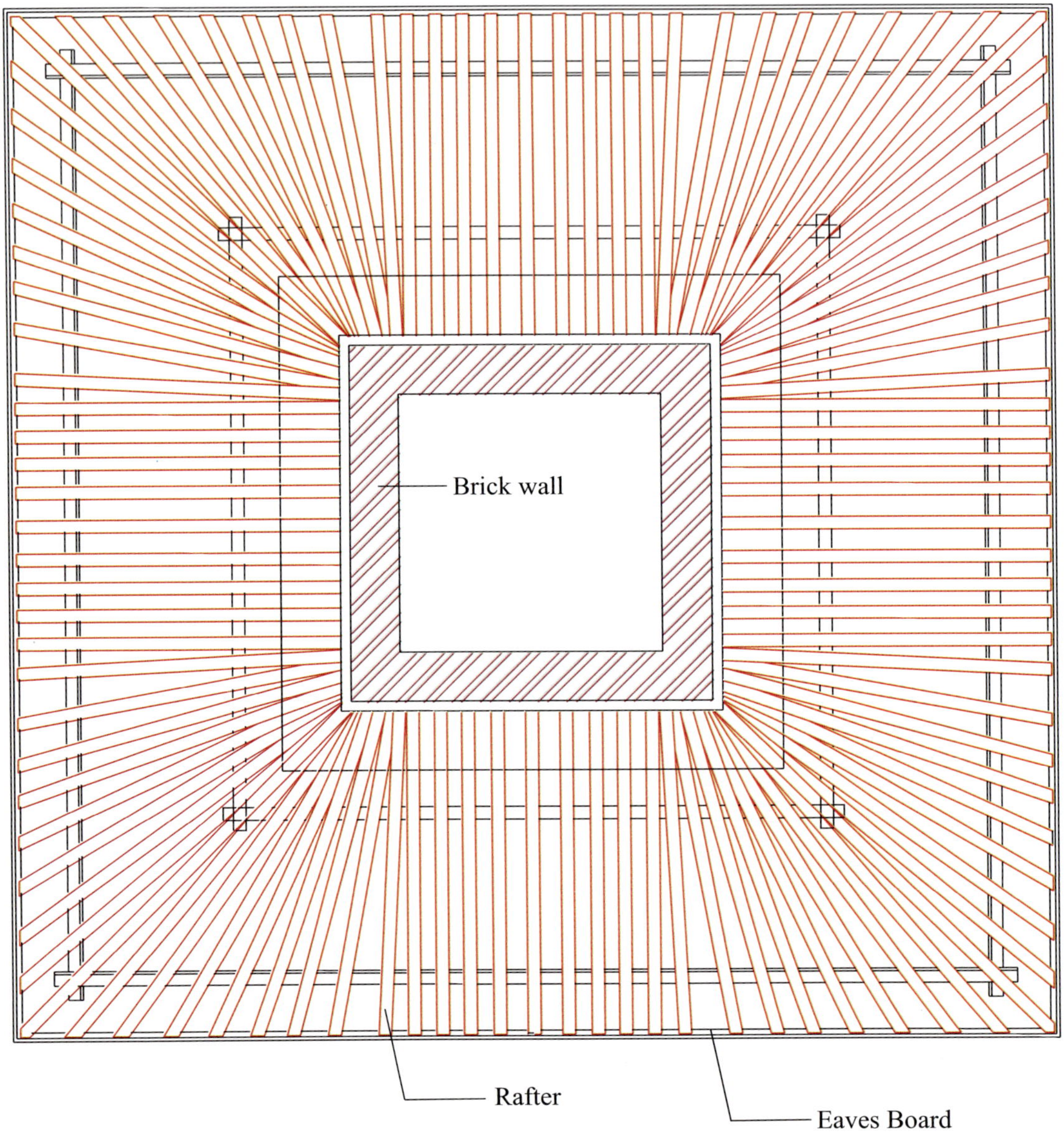

Figure 10. *Plan of Lower Roof Rafter of Maju Dega at Durbar Square, Kathmandu*

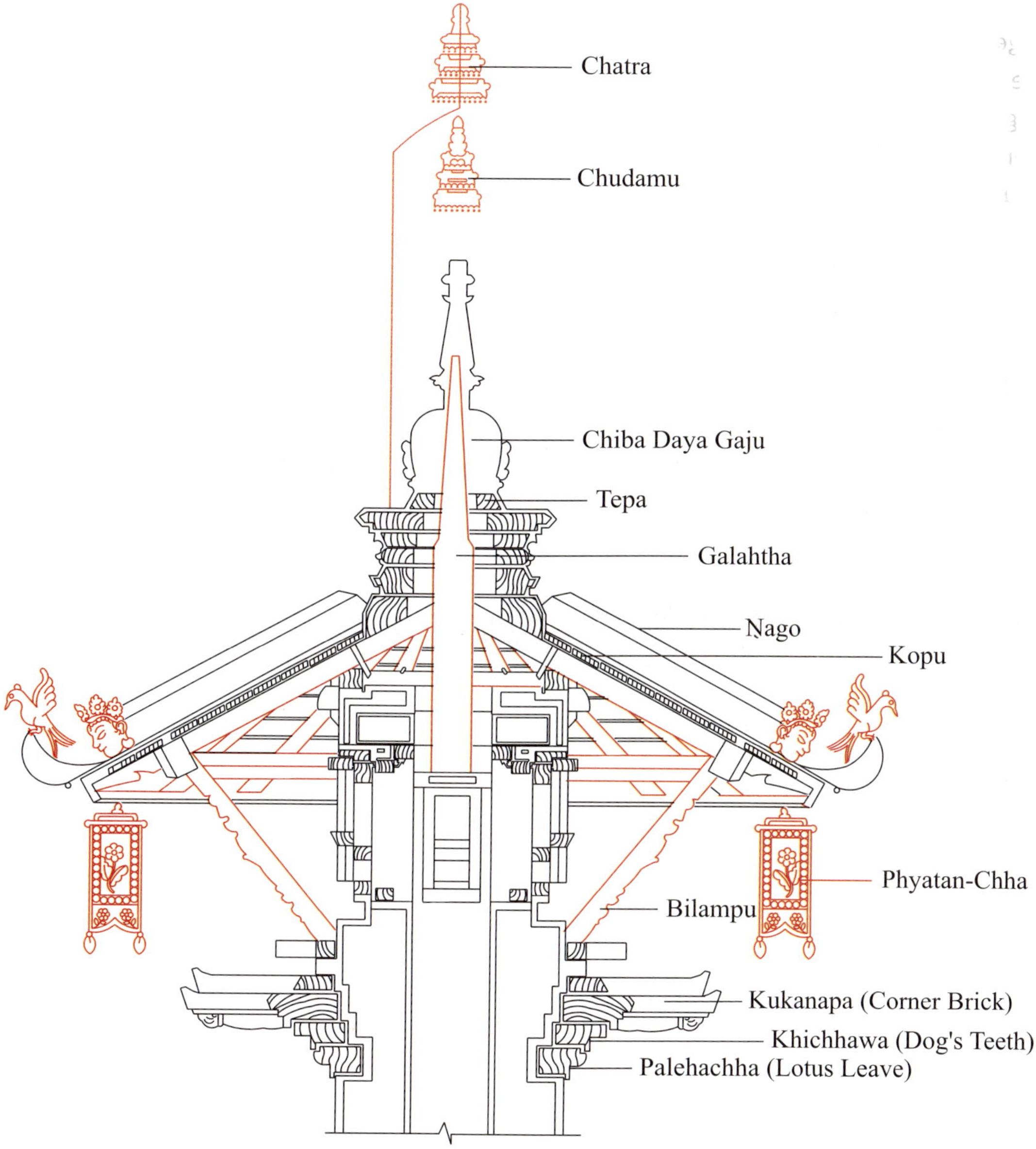

Figure 11. *Section of Top Roof Lokeshwore Mandir Tapalachi, Bhaktaput*

Another roof element which is almost universally found in Nepal, both on gilded and on tile roofs, is a border of bells. Bells 3 or 4 inches in length almost always hangs beneath the edge of overhanging roofs all around the temple. They are attached to small hooks below the roofs and have large metal clapper pendants which catches wind and cause the bells to ring in the breeze. These rows of bells all around the roof edges are a most essential element in giving Nepalese temple architecture its delicate appearance, even when the structure itself is massive and heavy.

Plate IV B. *Detail of Roof Boarder and Bell*

The roofs of the most elaborately metal-decorated temples often have hanging metal borders called *kihkimmala*, meaning "garland of little bells". They are solid or perforated and they are similar to the cloth hanging banners which are still to be seen on some temples. The metal hangings have motifs of bell elements, deity and various floral motifs. The borders are placed all along the undersides of the roofs, about 3 inches from the outer edges, and bells are often eliminated. Demon figures are sometimes seen on the borders as the protectors of the temple. Kathmandu's Matsyendranatha temple[1] has beautiful kihkimmala at both roof levels, with perforated designs of intertwining floral designs.

Hundreds of tiny bronze pendants are attached to the lower edge of the *kihkinimala* here, shimmering in the light and breeze.

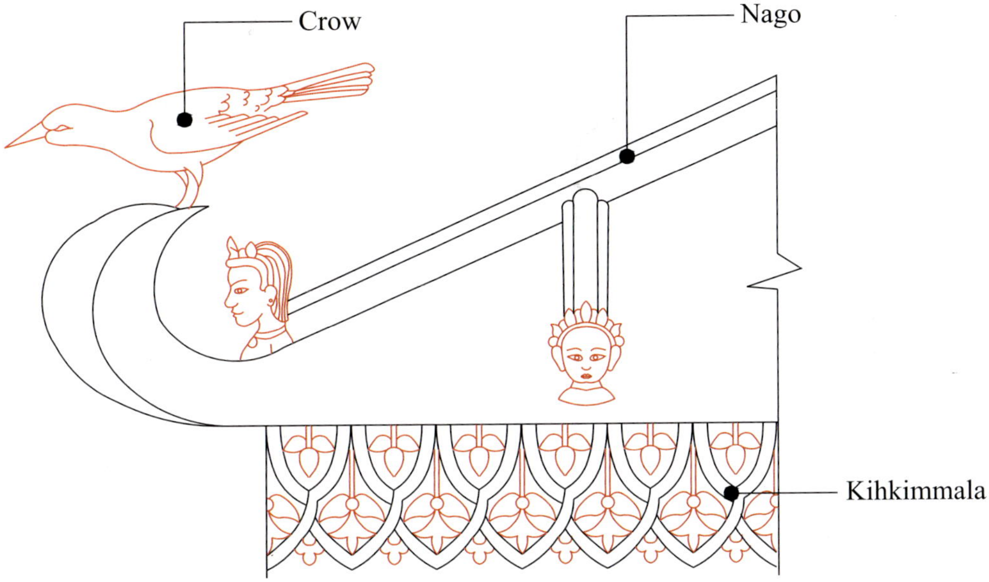

Elevation of Roof Corner with Border

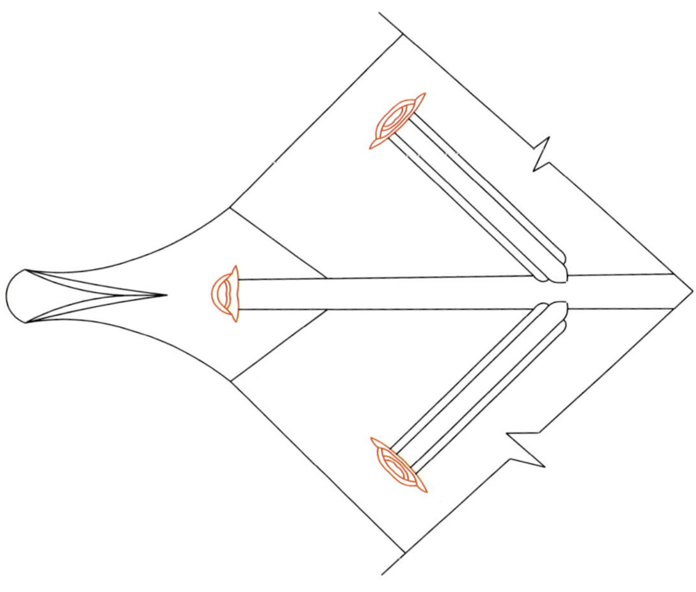

Figure 12. *Plan of Roof Corner*

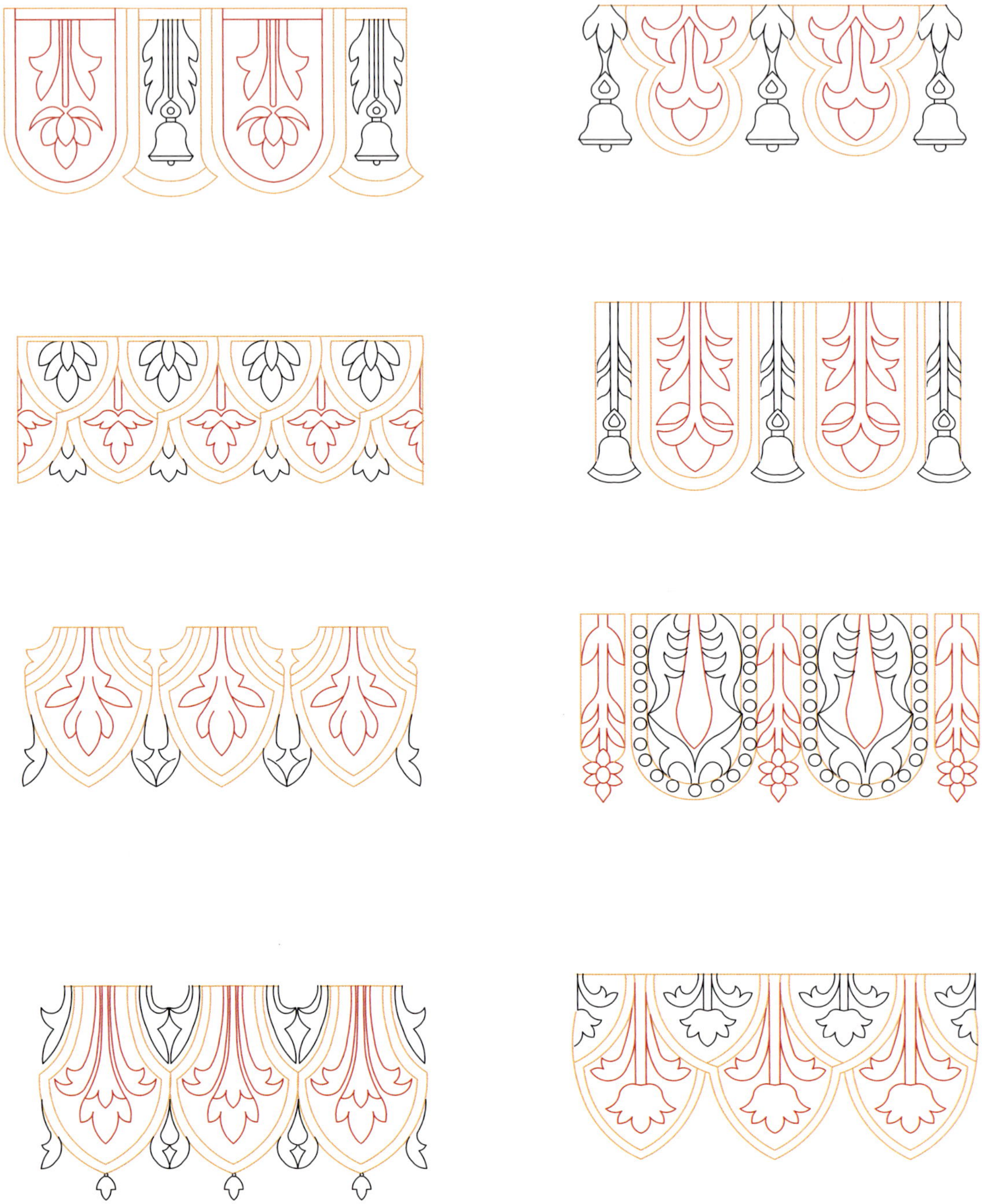

Figure 13. *Elevation of Different Types of Boarder (Libicha) (Y.R. Bajracharya)*

The figure of four major gods of great power is also placed in four cardinal directions to avoid the invading hoards of irreligious, evil spirits and fear. These four major gods are hanged diagonally at four corners so that they can be seen easily and protect the temple. The four figures of major gods are:

(i) Birudhaka holds a sword (Khadga) with his right hand and left hand rests on his knee. He is blue or green in colour.
(ii) Dhritrastra holds Vina and faces east. He is white in colour.
(iii) Vaisravana is also denoted as god of wealth and called Kubara. His right hand holds Citron (Banner) and mongoos by left hand. He is yellow in color.
(iv) Viropaksha holds chaitya with his left hand and serpent with his right hand. He is red in colour and faces west.

Descending Metal Banners—the *Pataka*

The long metal banners called *dhvajas* or *patakas*, which descend from the pinnacle down past the edge of the lowermost roof edge, are equally important from a religious and decorative point of view. These long ropeways of connected metal plates are said to be a kind of pathway for the gods to descend towards earth from heaven. This banner itself is not considered to be an essential temple attribute. Most of the temples do not have them but some have as many as four or five. They hang from the pinnacle and extend from the upper roof to the lowest roof over the main entrance. However, in some cases, the *pataka* descends only over the upper roof and not beyond that. The type of metal used in pataka are gold, silver or copper. The gold plated pataka are found in most of the huge temples. Silver pataka are mostly found inside the temple offered to God. Copper pataka is most common as it is cheaper in comparison. The eight auspicious symbols are the popular themes of design on these banners.

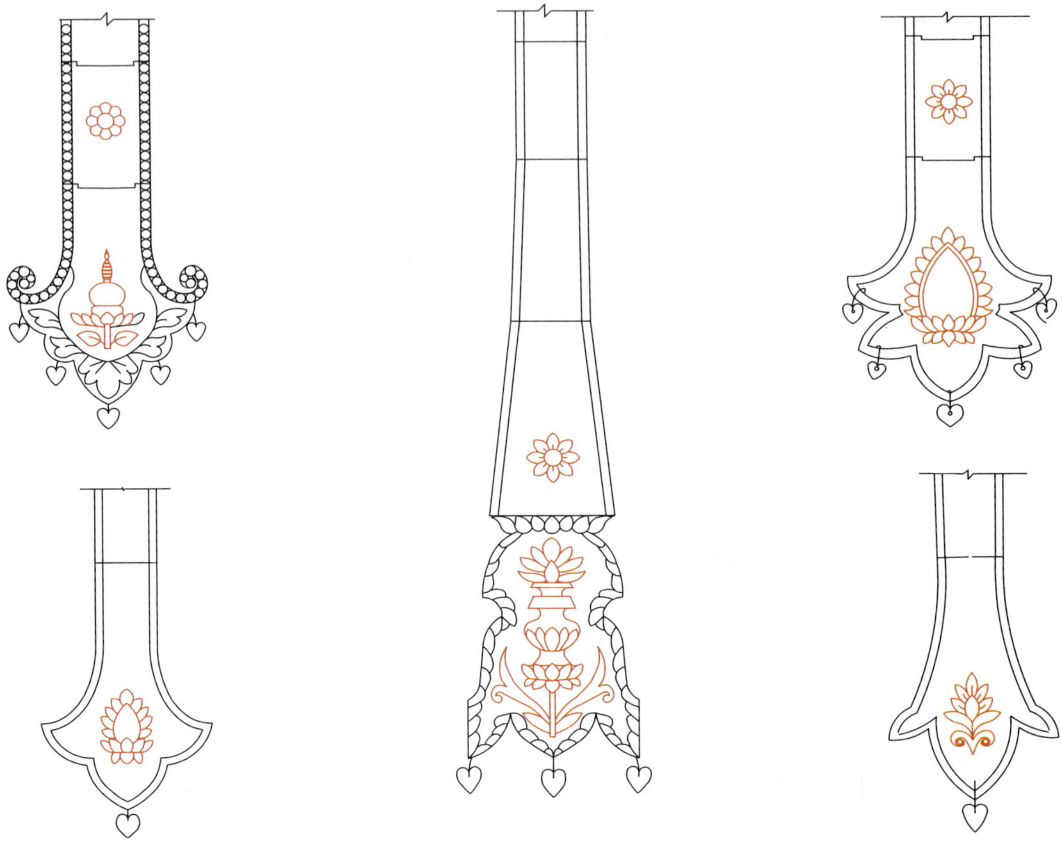

Elevation of Different Types of Banner (Pataka)

BILANPU

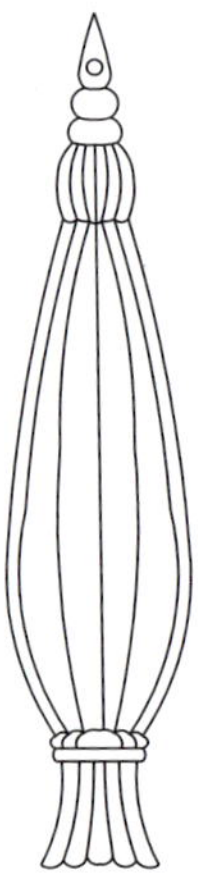

GOLODHIJA

BILANPU

Figure 14. *Elevation of Different Types of Banners (pataka) & Corner Hangings (Y.R. Bajracharya)*

Plate IV C. *Detail of Roof Descending Banner*

The three-storied temple of Vajra Yogini[2] has a banner extending from the pinnacle past the edge of the middle roof only, while the Bagh Bhairav of Kirtipur has a pataka extending from the pinnacle to just beyond the uppermost roof. The length of the banners usually depends upon the resources of those who donate them and they probably are symbolically satisfying to the devotee regardless of their length.

Notes

1. Matsyendranatha Temple- This temple is two storied with double wall construction. It is square in plan and measures 27' x 27'. It is located in the heart of Kathmandu near Asan tole. This temple is dedicated to Lokeshore. This is one of the most elaborate decorative temple found in Nepal and is sacred to both Hindus and Buddhists.
2. Vajra Yogini Temple- The 17th century Vajrayogini Temple is located 1.5 km north of Sankhu (16 km from Kathmandu) in the northeast of Kathmandu District. It is dedicated to the tantric goddess Vajrayogini (also called Ugratara-Vajrayogini) who is the Hindu/Buddhist manifestation of the goddess Kali. The three-tiered Vajrayogini Temple still stands in its original state. A submission was made to UNESCO in 2008 to list it as a World Heritage Site.

Chapter 5

Strut

Struts in temples are basically a long wooden planks which support the overhanging roof of the temple. Struts are usually decorated with various carvings of gods, goddesses and animals. It transfers the load of the roof to the vertical load-bearing wall. The struts project upward and outward from the base of the cornice ledge to meet the overhanging roof. The struts are firmly braced against the wall of the temple core. They are in every practical sense a brace to prop up the roof which extends too far beyond the central core to support its own weight. Struts can be classified into two groups according to their position in the temple: one is side strut and other is corner strut. Side struts are usually between windows and corner struts. Basically they are even in number, forming odd bays. Corner struts, as the name indicates, lie in the four corners of the temple. Side struts consists of two types: (i).Struts with religious motifs (ii).Struts with semi religious motifs.

Struts of religious motifs consists of the figures of the Tantric Deities, Shiva and his forms like Bhairava, Shiva-Paravati, Vishnu and his ten incarnations, Lokeswaras, Bodhisatwas, Astamatrika and gods like Varuna and Agni.

Struts of the second type consist of the representations of mythological figures like those of Bhimasena, gods associated with the constellations, Salabhanjika, etc.

Strut is generally divided into three portions top portion, middle portion and bottom portion with respect to its carving. The base and top portion of the struts are usually separated from the middle portion as they are plainer than the middle portion. The top portion consists of tree branches with heavy foliage hanging down and serves as a background of the main figure. Base portion is carved with the shape of rocks, foliage or the separate scenes related with the main image of the struts but more commonly they consist of scenes of sexual subjects. The erotic scenes are mostly associated with the Shiva temple. The monasteries are generally devoid of them. Erotic carvings are normally associated with the structure of the late seventeenth century.

The middle portion is the main part forming 50% or more of its total length, and nearly

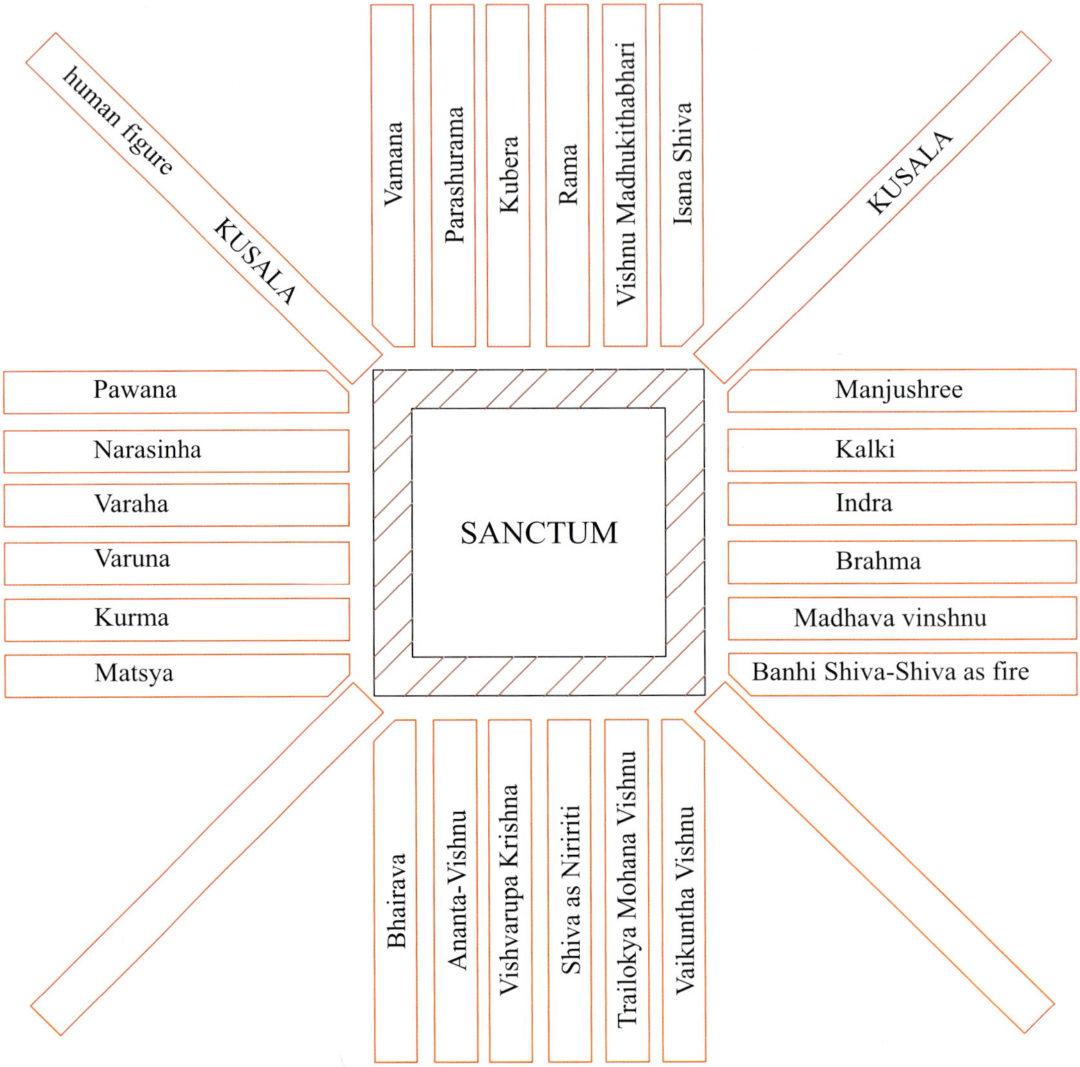

Figure 15. *Plan of Lower Level Struts of Changu Narayan Temple*

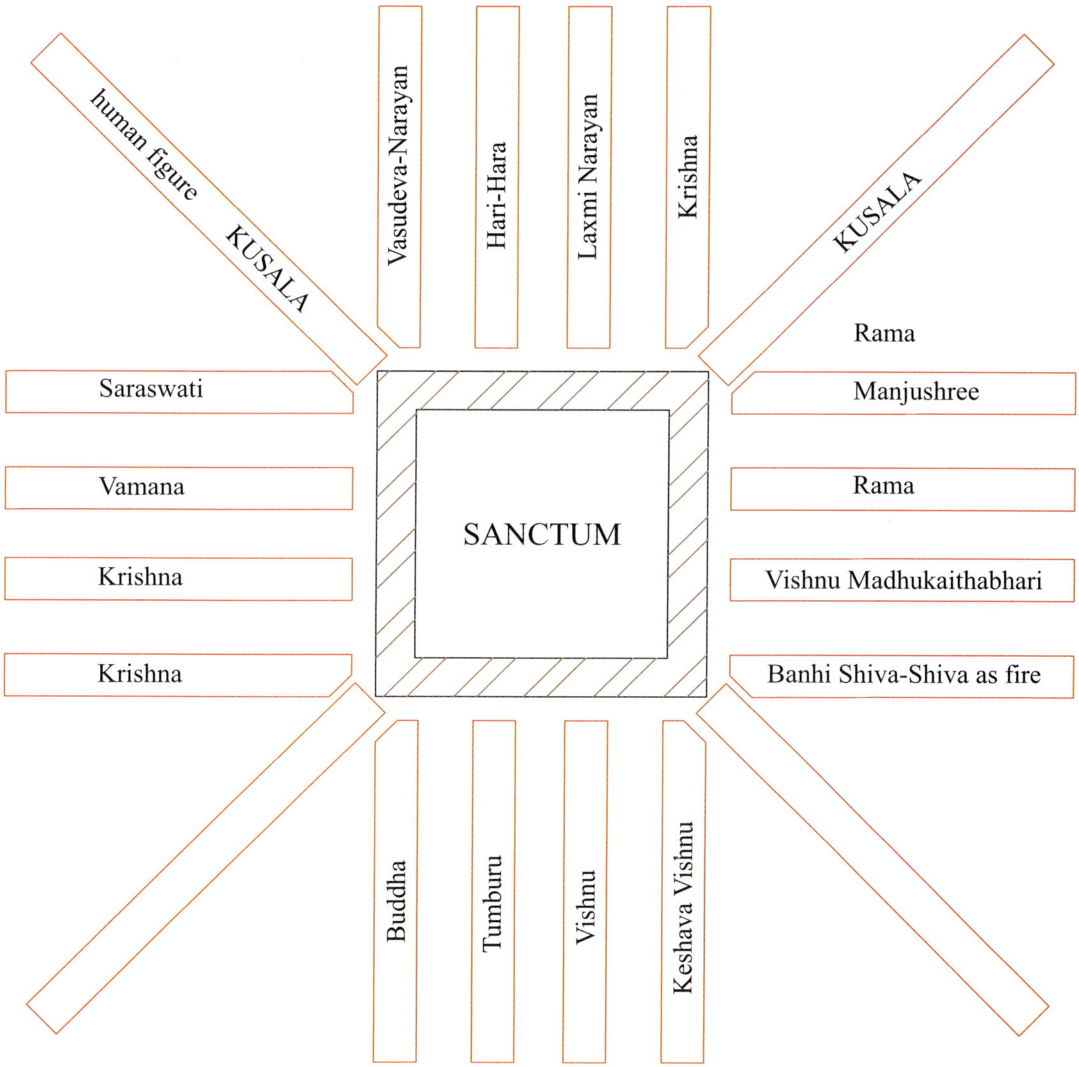

Figure 16. *Plan of Upper Level Struts of Changu Narayan Temple*

always holds a three-dimensional image of a god mounted on a base supported by attendants, human or animals. The size of deities on the middle portion of the struts ranges from 2 feet in small temples to 5 or 6 feet in large temples. It consists of gods and goddesses in various postures and colours mostly related with the god enshrined in the temple.

In most Buddhist temples many of the carved images of gods are identical in every respect except for colours. Their hue is of directional significance within the cosmic map that is the pantheon of deities. In other parts of the temple like in cornice, colour may in fact be merely decorative but at the struts level it is employed for iconographic identity.

Their postures usually have the legs crossing each other so that the forward foot rests on its toes while the straight leg behind it has its foot flattened atop the base or vehicle. The posture of legs of the deity has different symbolization, alidh asana and pratyalidh asana. Alidh asana (when right leg is positioned upward) meaning starting of work and pratyalidh asana (when left leg is positioned upward) meaning the completion of work.

The deity facing front has its arms, almost always multiple in number extending out from the body to display various symbols held in the hands. A representation of Shiva, for example, almost always holds a trident (trishul) in one hand and some other objects in other hands, while Vishnu grasps a conch shell (sankha) in his hand. The arms are usually of separate attachments while the rest of the figure is carved from a single block of wood. The pairing of deities such as Shiva and Parvati is critical to the tantric belief of power coming from the male and female union. These pair of deities in single struts are found supporting the bottom roof struts while single male figures (Vishnu, Bhairav) on the middle roof struts and single female figures (Astamatrika) on top roof struts. The Lokeshwara, the tantric form of Shiva and Parvati, Vishnu and Laxami, Indra and Indrayani, ten incarnations of Vishnu, Astramatrika, Dikpal, etc. are carved on these struts. In some temples extra narrow strut beams of red and blue floral design are placed on either side of every strut on a lower level. For example, in Dakshin Kali mandir situated in west side of royal palace Kathmandu, there are eight representations of Bhairava on the struts of the first level, and figures of Kali, Indrayani, Kumari, Visnavi, Mahesvari, Brahmayani, Kumar, and Ganesha. These figures are always shown with their various attendants (vehicle) like the peacock, bull, goose, etc.

The heavy corner struts where deity figures are absent are replaced by very powerful beasts or leogryphs. These corner animals, which are very unique in structure and quite heavy to move, are symbols of structural stability of Nepalese temple architecture. Such struts are traditionally carved with very fierce-looking animals that represents divine strength to keep the temples safe. These animals are generally seen below the corners of the overhanging roofs because they are considered to be very strong to keep even the heaviest roofs from collapsing and also equally capable of guarding the temples from the destructive forces of evil spirits. These fascinating animals, always shown in pairs, two males and two females, seem to wear a very serious composite look of three different animals-horse, goat and lion. These unique creatures have the face of a highly spirited-faced horse, incredibly curved horns of wild mountain goat and above all a symmetrical body of a fairly big size lion. Apart from this, the front and hind legs with extending sharp claws and mysterious flaming wings shooting up from all four legs of the creature plus the mouth and tail definitely add a lot of colour and character to its personality without any clear concern for colour symbolism as in the figures of deities. Its imposing appearance in a very wild and watchful attitude is ferocious enough to scare any offender from the temple premises. Corner struts of lower level of Indraswore temple[1] at Panauti have size of 3.90 m x 30 cm x 30 cm. Temples notable for the outstanding carving of their struts are Changu Narayana, Nyatapola in Bhaktapur, Jaganath[2] in Kathmandu.

In the temple of Changu Narayan there are 24 struts in lower roof level and 16 struts in upper roof levels. The figures in struts are different incarnations of Vishnu. Careful examination of the struts of Changu Narayan reveals that there is lack of erotic images so commonly found on struts of Nepalese temple. In the place of human or animal beings engaged in sexual plays, one finds the benign images of a rishi beneath the feet of each of the torana deities. The rishis are thus believed to be iconograhic remnants of the original temple struts. The deities represented on the struts of lower and top level of the Changu Narayan temple listed from left to right are as follows (Jeff Lidke).

East Side

Lower Level

a. Banhi Shiva Shiva as fire
b. Madava Vishnu
c. Brahma
d. Indra
e. Kalki
f. Manjushri

Upper Level

a. Balarama (Ananta)
b. Dhamodhara Vishnu
c. Hari Hara
d. Shesha

West Side

Lower Level

a. Pawana
b. Narasinha
c. Varaha
d. Varuna
e. Kurma
f. Matsya

Upper Level

a. Saraswati
b. Vamana
c. Krishna
d. Krishna

South Side

Lower Level

a. Bhairava
b. Ananta-Vishnu
c. Vishwarupa Krishna
d. Shiva as Niririti
e. Trailokya Mohana Vishnu
f. Vaikuntha Vishnu

Upper Level

a. Buddha
b. Tumburu
c. Vishnu
d. Keshava Vishnu

North Side

Lower Level

a. Isana Shiva
b. Vishnu Madukaithabhari
c. Rama
d. Kubera
e. Parashurama
f. Vamana

Upper Level

a. Krishna
b. Lakshmi-Narayana
c. Hari Hara
d. Vasudeva-Narayana

The eight corner struts are the biggest as they have the most weight to carry. The mythical figures on these struts are a griffin with the face of a male bird's wing and a lion's body. Despite their continual replacement due to natural damage, the arrangement of the struts is not random; it follows closely the systematic rules of tantric iconography.

The deities of eight mother Goddesses (***Asta Matrikas***) are the most common in the struts of Hindu temple. The hindus look upon the eight mother goddess as their protector. Carvings of Astrimatrika in struts are found in the temple of Taleju in Kathmandu, Naxal Bhagbati[3], Indrayani Temple[4] in the bank of Bishnumati river and Ekalakhu Ganesh at Patan. They wear multi-coloured costumes and ornaments, have several arms and have symbolic vehicles. Rudrayani or Vajrayani on a bull, Brahmayani on a goose, Vaishnavi on Garuda, Indrayani on an elephant, Kumari on a peacock, Chamunda or Kali on a demon, Varahi on a buffalo and Mahalakshmi on a lion. They are easily recognized by their vehicles or vahanas which are usually animals or birds. The images of Asta Matrikas goddesses with their colour, vehicle and number of hands are given in Table 5.1. These images of Matrika goddesses are found installed in various places of the Kathmandu Valley.

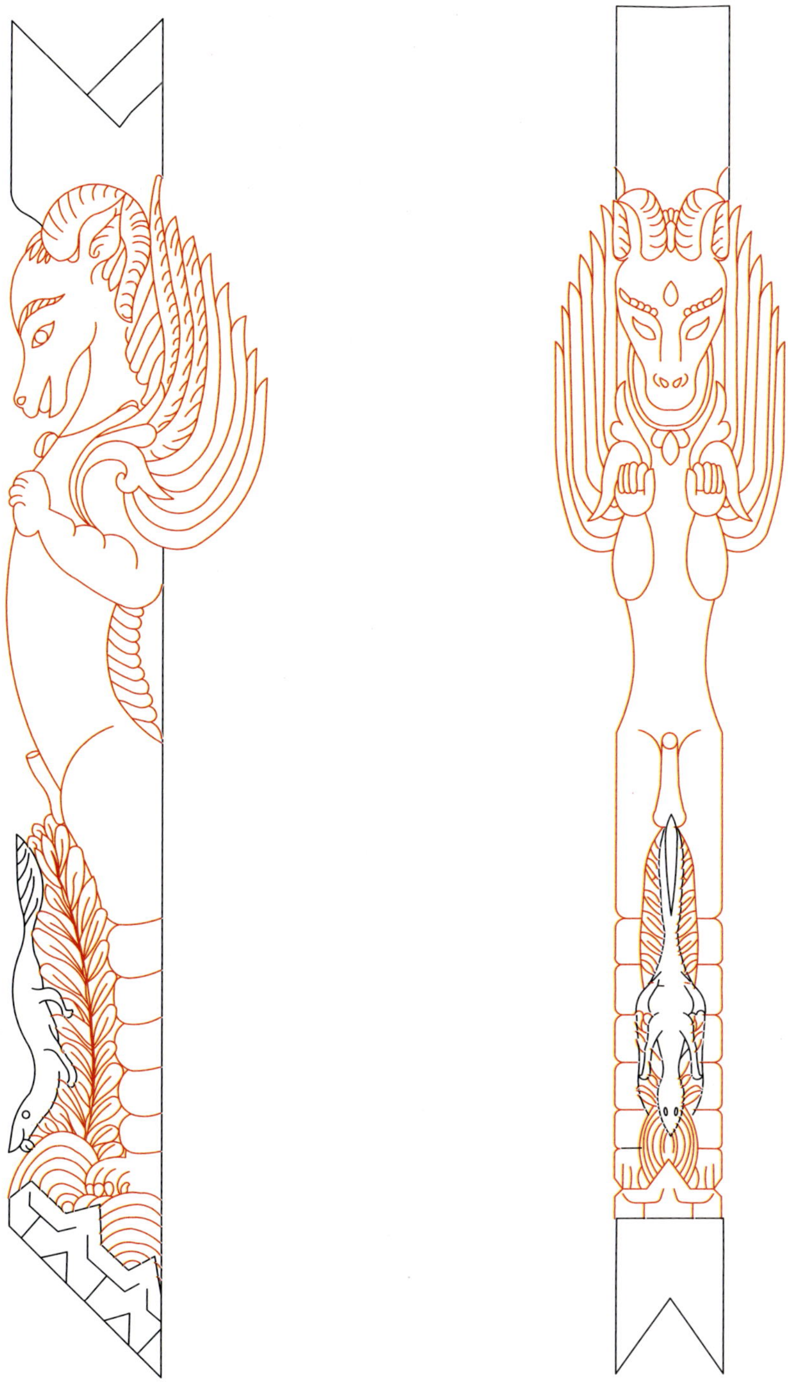

SIDE ELEVATION FRONT ELEVATION

Figure 17. *Corner Struts (Kusala)*
(Y.R. Bajracharya)

Figure 18. *Middle Struts (Y.R. Bajracharya)*

Plate V A. *Lower Roof Strut of Changu Narayan Temple (Ananta Vishnu) South Side*

Plate V B. *Lower Roof Strut of Changu Narayan Temple (Bhairava) South Side*

Plate V C. *Lower Roof Strut of Changu Narayan Temple (Parshurama) North Side*

STRUTS

Plate V D. *Lower Roof Corner Strut of Changu Narayan Temple*

Plate V E. *Lower Roof Strut of Changu Narayan Temple (Bishworoop Krishna) South Side*

STRUTS

Plate V F. *Lower Roof Strut of Changu Narayan Temple (Kubera) North Side*

Table 5.1.

S.N.	Name of God	Shakti	Colour	Vehicle	No. of Hands on struts of Shakti
1.	Rudra or Mahadeva	Rudrayani	White	Bull	She is a 4, 6 or 10-handed goddess. She holds a javelin and a rosary. Other two hands are boon-giving and protective poses. She has three eyes.
2.	Brahma	Brahmayani	Yellow	Goose	She has four hands. They carry a vase and a rosary, other two hands are in boon-giving and protective pose
3.	Vishnu	Vaishnavi	Green	Garuda/ Eagle	She is 4 or 6-handed. She carries a conch shell and a wheel in one hand. Other two hands are protective and boon-giving pose.
4.	Indra	Indrayani	Orange	Elephant	She is four-handed with two in boon-giving and protective poses. Two carries a spear and thunderbolt.
5.	Agni	Kumari	Red	Peacock	She is 2, 4 or 12-handed carries a spear and a cock. Two hands are in boon-giving and protection poses.
6.	Yama	Chamunda	Red	Demon/ Corpse Owl	She is 4 or 10-handed carries a goad, axe, sword and a trident.
7.	Varaha	Varahi	Red	Buffalo	She is boar-headed and 4-handed carries a plough and a spear in two hands. Other two hands are boon-giving and protective pose.
8.	Kuware	Mahalakshmi	Red	Lion	She is two-handed and her hands are in *abhaya mudra* and *varada mudra* (protection and boon-giving postures).

When Ugrachandi is added to the above list they become *Navdurga* or nine mother goddesses.

The identification of the many gods and goddess in struts is a very complex problem. As an aid to its identification emblem and carrier of different gods and goddesses are given in the Appendix1, 2 & 3.

Notes

1. Indraswore Temple- This temple is situated in Panauti and is of two storeys. It was built in 13th century. This temple is dedicated to rain god Indra. In this temple struts supporting the roof of Indraswore temple have the hands of the deties within the frame. It is square in plan with its dimension measuring 12.59mx 12.59m and has height of 20.35 m including pinth.
2. Jaganath Temple- This is a two tiered temple located in Kathmandu Durbar square. It was built by Mahendra Mall in 1563A.D.. This temple rest on three palteform and has two tired roof supported by some elaborately carved roof struts of erotic figures. Each of four elevations contains groups of three doors that are of excellent quality. The central door in each case carries the signs of Mahadev,three eyes and a trident and on each of other door are symbols of the shakta cults to represent the goddess, three indentations above a decorative pot.
3. Naxal Bhagbati Temple- This is a three storied temple situated in Bhagavati Vahal of Naksal, Kathmandu. According to record, this temple was renovated in 1781A.D. The struts supporting the lowest roof have carvings of the eight matrikas and the eight Bhairabs.
4. Indrayani Temple- This temple was built in 1782 A.D.. This three storied temple of the Matrikas is located next to Bishnumati river. It has a carved struts which depicts the matrika goddesses and bhairavas. The sanctum contains no idols and only plain stones are used for worshipping according to Tantric tradition.

Chapter 6

Cornice and String Course

The cornice is the string course located at the base of the struts in every floor of temples. It marks the division of a temple into individual tier (stories).The cornice in temples is mostly of carved wooden border 1 to 2 feet wide. It has structural as well as ornamental significance in the temple. The top of the cornice usually has a brick ledge extending about 4 to 10 inches from the wall which serves as a base for the struts. These bricks are of large size and are projected from the core wall. The ledge bricks acts as a kind of pavement and prevents moisture from soaking into the cornice. The ledge brick is sometimes painted in red and yellow or red and white colour. In small temples wooden pieces are used instead of these bricks. Below the ledge brick wooden cornice is provided. This cornice band is provided with at least three layers:

(i) Chvúậ (mouse Teeth)
(ii) Dhalì.mvhậ (end of Joist)
(iii) Khicậvậ (dog's teeth) and Nag (snake).

The upper layer exhibits in most cases a pattern of mouse teeth (chúvậ).

The middle layer is the extension of inner joist which forms the ceiling within the inner shrine. These joists are carved in the shape of animal heads or demon heads or head of mythical birds. These joists extend about 3 to 6 inches from the rest of the cornice. These represent protectors of the temple and servants of the deities to which the temple is dedicated. These demon heads decrease in number from ground level to upper level. They are said to frighten malevolent spirits away from the temple and for this reason alone they are often made to look quite fierce, like the grinning skulls. Lotus flower and the symbol of Astamangala are carved in between these projected joists.

The lower layer consists of a snake (nậhg) pattern combined with dog's teeth (Khicậvậ). Besides these layers some other layers are added which are not fixed. The lowermost part of the cornice exhibits an egg (ậsa) or walnut (Khvahsigvah) pattern with frill or lotus flower.

These layers are not related to the interior structure of the temple and are simply one of the many traditional cornice borders.

Apparently, colour symbolism is less important in the painting of these cornice heads than of the carvings of deities in struts. Most often, they are unpainted. Patterns of decoration on wooden cornice in Mahadeva Temple in Pachali are mouse teeth, beam end with Kusuru head, dog's teeth, snake and lotus flower with alternating bell. If ever they are painted they are in five colours like white, blue, green, yellow and red. When the protruding elements of the cornice are left square and uncarved they are marked merely by painted flowers.

Plate VI A. *Cornice of Changu Narayan Temple South Side*

Both brick and wooden parts of the cornice extend beyond the corner of the temple, where they cross each other to reach into space as brick ends with upturned edges that resemble the curves placed at the corners of roofs. The underside of such brick is carved into the shape of human forearms with hands that support the brick. These are given

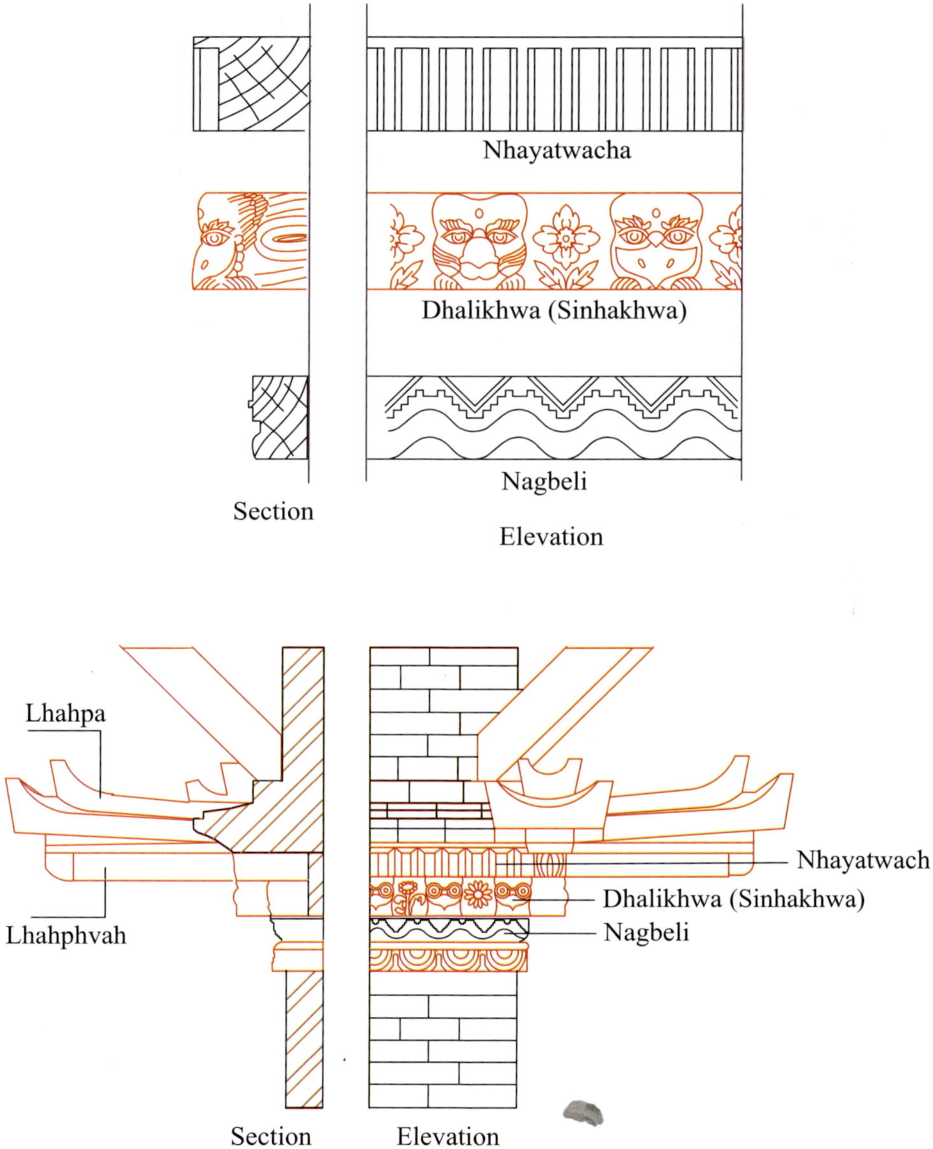

Figure 19. *Section & Elevation of Wooden Cornice (W. Korn)*

emphasis in temple design, almost always crossing over one another to project from 1 to 2 feet beyond the corners of the temple. They are effective visually and appropriate to the total design because the ends are broadened and then tapered upward in a form like the roof curve, giving the cornice a light appearance, but they are not as essential to the temple scheme like the roof forms without which the temple superstructure would seem oppressively heavy.

Plate VI B. *Cornice Detail at Corner of Pachali Mahadeva Temple*

The extended brick end consists of two or three layers, each shorter than the one below it, all ending in an upward curve. These corner bricks are of the biggest size among other bricks used in the temple. They are specially moulded and are known as lhậhpậ. It is interesting to note that wooden arms of human shape are quite often carved below the extended beams, palm upward, as if to support the bricks. The hand usually forming a fist may be painted red like the bricks of the wall or cornice, with white outlining around the edges. The forms of lotus leaves, a flower, frill and half lotus are usually carved below the ends of the joist level timber band in different combinations.

Chapter 7

Windows

Windows in temples are placed at the centre of building façade in each direction on upper levels. Windows are odd in number and are axially symmetrical in plan. It is customary to have at least one window on each side of each storey between the struts. These windows are firmly mounted into the core wall and have no openings in the brick wall behind the window. They are often decorative rather than functional. The windows are either latticed or are finished with vertical blinds containing an image. Window openings have a permanent grilled screen. The grill work of window openings mostly has a diamond or square shape. As a part of decoration the head of a god or that of an animal vahana of a main deity is carved in the centre of the window.

Each window consists of two frames, inner frame (Duchue) and the outer frame (Bha) both of which are held together by wooden nail and wooden ties. The inner frame is larger than the outer frame. The outer frame of window is often enormously carved. The sill and lintel are made longer for structural purpose. On both sides, arched panels flushed on the wall are kept for supporting the lintel. The top of the lintel has several receding brick course called mikhaphusi (eyebrow). Lintels and Jambs are often composed of parallel miniature wooden member decorated with linear patterns of foliage, flower, beads, animals, birds and often with figures of deities or mythological scenes.

The general classification of windows is based on several aspects of windows such as the number of openings and the way they are attached to the wall and the types of window frames and the way they are supported. Most common windows used in temple are: **Ga Jhayậ** (Blind Window), **Pashukha Jhyậ** (row of small windows).

Ga Jhyậ is a blind window specially used in the temples. It is constructed with secondary jambs and forward standing posts (Tvaltha). The middle opening, however, is divided by a sill. The lower part is closed by an apron plank (Jhyakvatah) fixed into a frame, the upper part has an extra frame with a figure of a god. On the second floor of Changu Narayan temple each window on all four sides has the figure of Vishnu. It has a vertically rectangular opening with lintel extended and the wings depicting various motifs like a winged horse, a lion or a deity standing in tribhanga. It is a single bay window (chappa Jhyậ) and has the image of a god at the centre, usually Bhairab. The upper corners of extended lintels are carved with leaves and flowers.

Plate VII A. *Gha Jhyậ of Bajrayogni Temple*

Pashukya Jhyậ is a monastic window, which has three to five openings. The openings are odd in number mostly 3 or 5. The central opening usually more decorated than others has double shutter whereas the rest of the openings have single shutter. Usually windows have rectangular forms and the ratio of length and breadth are 3:1, or 5:1. Mostly Pashukya Jhayậ is located in first floor of the temple. In Newari language, pashukya denotes a long religious five fine threads essential material for religious rituals. It is also believed that the five sets of openings denote these five threads.

Just above the openings is again a long lintel type of timber member carved longitudinally in receding pattern. This member assures the protection of openings from rainwater. The bottom of lintel frame has square or trapezoidal patterns above the window opening. The jambs of the openings are carved to imitate pilasters with moulding of Kalasha Motifs at the middle or at the bottom, decorated with carvings of leaves on the sides. Among various carvings lined in the jambs, lotus motif is easily recognizable.

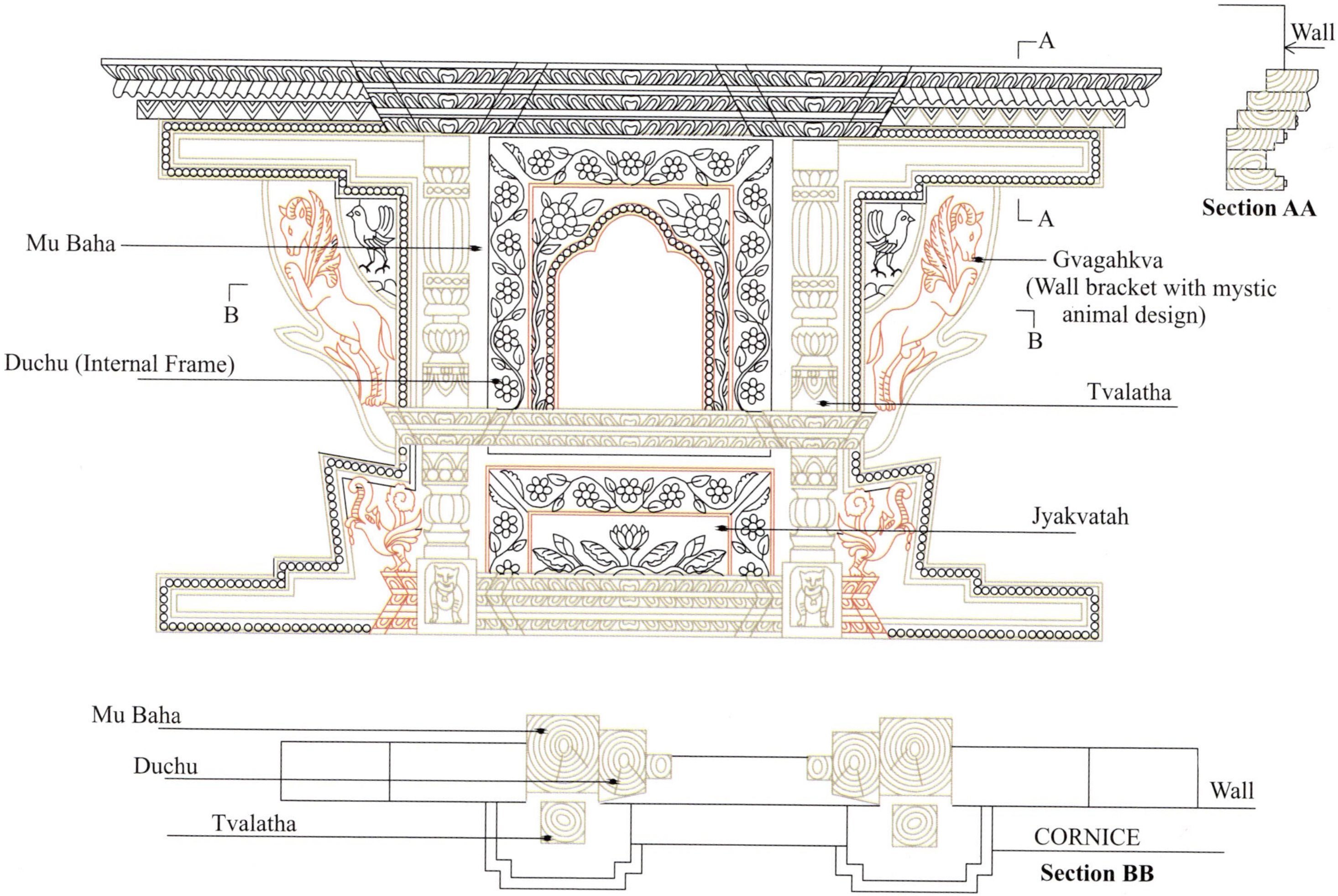

Figure 20. *Typical Elevation & Section of Ga-Jhya*

Moldings on free-standing column (Tvalatha) on each side of opening have a prescribed formula: square blocks at the top and bottom, a round central shaft, and a symbolic ring of amalaka fruit representing the celestial world above and hinting at the primordial tree that bears fruit of that shape.

Plate VII B. *Pashuka Jhyḙ̂ of Kasi Bishwonath Temple, Bhaktapur*

A kalasha is always found below, filled with water and overflowing with vegetation; it is the vase of plenty on which the pillar rests. An octagonal cross-section makes a formal transition between the square above and round forms below.

The sides of openings are again carved with beads. Almost every part is carved except the sill member and the shutters. The base of the central posts has lion images. The lower corners of the sill member have Makara or crocodile image, which represents one of the five eternal elements of water.

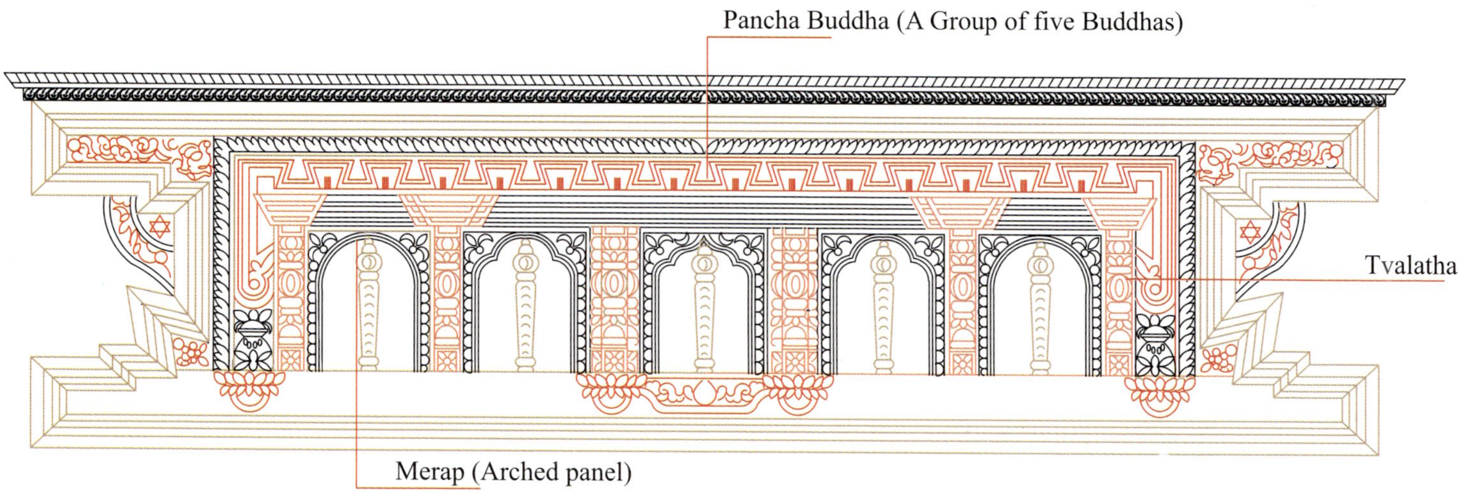

Figure 21. *Elevation of Pashuka Jhaya (C.B.Joshi)*

Symbolic carvings in windows are in general auspicious which are the peacocks, nagas, lotus flowers and vajra (thunderbolts) but the representation of major gods is a very rare part of its scheme. Symbols such as the lotus and *purna kalasa* are occasionally mounted into the window frame.

Window frames also have wings attached to their jambs and have carvings of Kumsalas or leogryphs. The angular extensions at the base of windows are decorated with flowers and carved with guardians like on the door. This is perhaps because the windows are not in need of protection. The windows are enclosed by many frames and lintels which are of multiple parts like that of the doors. The lintel of the frame is commonly of dentil type but it holds a nail heads border of three-dimensional diamond cuts. It is of multiple lintel type or quite plain. The ledge below is sometimes carved to include the nearly free-standing figures of Surya and his team of solar horses, or takes the form of a kind of false balcony adorned with peacocks, snakes, and dragons. It is screened and has a semi-circular base.

In addition to image-holding window frames, small wooden niches mounted in the core walls beside the windows and doors hold small figures of deities.

Niches

Niches are similar to windows and are of smaller size, usually about 2 feet in height by 18 inches in width. Niches are usually placed at either side of doors and windows. Niches do not have extended beams at the lintel and sill to anchor them into the brick wall.

Niches have torana that is carved in the usual way and mounted so as to slant forward from the wall. Below its sill there is an extra half-circle of wood which is reverse in shape of torana but its carving is not similar to the torana. Carving in this holds entwined flowers and leaves at its centre with several decorative borders leading to an outer enclosure that resembles the border of the torana. Besides, it also has carvings of Yantra, lotus (Palahah) or snake virgin (Nagkanaya). The frame of the niche as a whole is nearly as variable in form as that of the window, with small frames being carved into the shape of lotus blossoms with the opening of the niche contained within their petals. The semi-circular base is a differentiating feature which is usually found in blind window and not in other type of windows. These blind windows don't seem to have any functional requirement since they are closed.

Plate VII C. *Niche of Bajrayogni Temple*

Figure 22. *Elevation of Niche at Chandeswore Temple, Banepa*

The niche exists to hold an image or symbol and these objects frequently represent the deity to whom the temple is dedicated. The very origin of its inclusion in the temple plan is in fact, due to the need to erect cult images at each of the cardinal points of early temples. The niche may also contain images of a lesser god's attendant to the main deity, or fierce guardians. The images are usually of wood or stone, although they are sometimes made of bronze or gilt-copper.

Plate VII D. *Niche of Pachali Mahadeva Temple*

Images of the niches are to re-emphasize the symbolic reference of the temple scheme and to provide extra objects of veneration at the lower level of the temple, where it can be easily approached by devotees. At upper levels, niches display the attendants of the main deity, especially beside central windows that often hold carvings or metal images of the main god himself or open into the holy space that is his inner shrine.

Since most worshippers are not allowed to enter the main shrine, the tiny bronze figure at the ground level is for devotion at this temple. The devotee may touch the symbol of the god with his own hands rather than pass offerings to a priest as intermediary or toss his gifts into a shadowed interior.

Chapter 8

Torana

A torana is a semi-circular, flat object made of wood or wood plated with metal, placed above the doorways in the temple. It usually leans slightly forward from the temple over the entrance opening or over a window. It is a separate object quite different from other parts of the door frame. Its base rests upon the cornice projection of the lintel above the door, and it is usually attached to the wall behind it by a chain or rope. It varies in size from small objects about 12 inches long that are placed over niches to major door carvings more than six feet wide at the base. In some temples torana is placed over all doors, windows and between columns. In Bishwonath temple[1] of Patan toranas are placed between columns (Plate VIII A). When its size big different boards are stacked horizontally and attached to each other without any gap to give a feeling of a single piece of wood. The internal pattern of the torana is stylistically consistent whether it is attached to a Hindu or Buddhist shrine. The main deity to whom the particular temple is dedicated usually represented at its centre. In all cases it stands as an auspicious object of great veneration, beauty, and elaboration, signifying that the building upon which it is placed is a sanctuary. It often has a number of miniature deities in niches evenly spaced upon the *torana* background, but are also covered by an extremely complex conglomeration of nagas (snakes), minor deities, animals, devotees, floral motifs, etc. Carved scenes in wooden toranas are usually very brightly painted and colour symbolism is not as important here as on struts.

Plate VIII A. *Torana Above the Column of Bishwonath Temple, Patan*

The common images carved in torana besides the central deity are:

(i) Chhepu a fierce beast placed at the top of torana which is in attitude of biting or holding snake as if attempting to escape. This indicates a strong sense of dedication to his duty. Holding of snakes, wearing its necklace and armbands symbolizes victory over his arch enemies.

(ii) Ganga a goddess representing holiest river always stands on a mythical sea monster (makara). Makara is more of a symbol of a perennial source of life than a mere decorative piece of art.

(iii) Jammuna a goddess also representing holiest river always stands on a tortoise (Kachuwa).

(iv) Apsaras an angelic female figure holding garlands in their hands.

Symmetry is maintained no matter how many extra figures or ornamental details are added to the torana, but floral motifs do much to bring freedom and movement to the whole composition. It is often capped by a gilt-copper finial. Flower patterns usually fill the oddest background space or the most irregular boarder area like in torana of Bagh Bhairav temple in Kirtipur (Plate VIII D). The same motif is seen in metal at temples such as the Haritimata shrine at Swayambhu, while the wooden representations are typical and found on almost any Nepalese temple. Matsyendranatha temple[2] in Patan has one of Nepal's most elaborate torana complexes with so much bronze ornamentation that the semi-circular torana shapes are almost lost in the ornamental setting.

Plate VIII B. *Torana Above the Golden Gate South Side Bhaktapur*

The golden gate of Bhaktapur had been described by historian Percy Brown as one of the most beautiful pieces of art in the whole kingdom of Nepal. The main attraction of this gate is the torana placed above the door (Plate VIII B). The torana is entirely of metal with the goddess Taleju at the centre. This triple-headed goddess has many arms modeled in very high relief and is accompanied by two standing attendants on either side. Over this trio is a border with figures of Garuda with coiling serpents and floral motifs. At the bottom of this border is Ganga and Jamuna. Ganga and Jamuna are holding Sinhamoo (ceremonial vermillio container) and Jwalanhyekan (ceremonial metal mirror) respectively. The design of the torana itself is often so involved that a photograph attached to this is a much more useful means of description than words.

Figure 23. *Elevation of Torana*

Figure 24. *Elevation of Torana*

Torana of Changu Narayan temple is also made up of metal with the god Bishnu at the centre and a figure of goddess Laxmi at the right side and figures of Garuda at the left side. On top of the torana, there is a terrific face of Garuda consuming a naga at each side of his mouth (Plate VIII C).

Plate VIII C. *Torana Above the Entry Door of Changu Narayan Temple West Side*

Another fine example of wood carving in torana is of Bagh Bhairava in Kirtipur. This torana is placed above the sacrificial altar on the left side of the main entrance. Torana is assembled with different pieces of wood (Plate VIIIC). It stands on a pair of wooden posts and is supported by a chain from behind. It has the central figure of Bagh Bhairava with Ganesh on the left side and Kumar on the right side. Above the central figure is Lord Narayana riding Garuda's shoulder with eight mother goddesses on both side. Eight mother goddesses and their consorts the eight Bhairavas are carved inside roundels forming outer border to the arch. Garuda holds a vessel (kalasa) with his two front hands and his two arms are spread out under his flying wings. Garuda also holds two nagkanya (women in the form of snakes from the waist down) in his claw on both sides. Mala, a creature of lightning in Newari, is carved below Ganesh and Kumar. There are two Hitimangah at each end of the torana, and two small flying griffins next to it.

Plate VIII D. *Torana, Above the Sacrifical Alter of Bagh Bhairav Temple, Kirtipur*

Among Torans in Kathmandu Valley there is no particular figure within the complex forms moulded upon the torana which may be exclusively Buddhist or exclusively Hindu. The only common element of the torana in both Hindu and Buddhist is the large central deity with or without attendants.

Chapter 9

Door and Doorframes

The doors of Nepalese temples, like those of dwellings, are quite small. They are rarely 5 feet high, and one must step over a wooden ledge 6 to 12 inches in height which blocks the lower part of the opening so one need to mind one's head while entering the temple. Nepalese temple doors have double shutters which are secured by a massive lock at the bottom where it meets the ledge and is secured by two short chains attached to the doors. Doors which are kept permanently or semi-permanently closed are sealed or locked from within, usually with the same kind of locks and chains as used on the exterior. A moulding mounted on one of each pair of doors makes it necessary to close one door before the other and leaves no crack or opening through which it would be possible to peep in. Temple door shutters are frequently filled with perforated screens of wood in a variety of patterns, but they are sometimes covered over with embossed metal or even left quite plain without even a peephole in each. The openings are usually rectangular in form but some doors have curved arches. The large eyes that are painted upon the panels of the door symbolize as the all-seeing eyes of the Buddha in a Buddhist context and the eyes of Shiva among Hindus. Door is of single bay type or triple bay type.

Simple door frames consist of a threshold, a pair of jambs and a lintel. The shape of the doorframe is remarkable. Similar to the window, the door frame consists of interior frame (Duchậ) and exterior frame (Bah) which are joined together with wooden nails (Chukuls). Exterior frame is for decorative purpose whereas inner frame is for structural purpose. The upper and lower beams of the standard frame of door extend far out into the brick wall, presumably for added strength. The upper beam of door frames are longer than the lower beams and the extensions reaches out almost to the corners of the brick core, forming a kind of continuous broad border all around the structure. The plane of door frame fits to the plane of the wall surface. The outer frame, decorated and stepped surrounds the whole door and bridges the gap between the surface of the wall and the level of the bearing frame. The design and iconography of the door frame reveals a theme of water cosmology in its

Plate IX A. *Door of CharNarayan Temple, Patan*

iconography and multiplied rectilinear forms in its physical shape. Door frames are usually decorated in some manner but their carvings are not as symbolic as those of the torana or struts. The door jambs also contain either at the base or at the centre, several deities like Bhairava, Vaisnava, Shiva or tantric male or female figure.

Outer door frame can be grouped into five categories according to decoration as shown in fig. 25.

(1). Gvậgahkvậ
(2). Debikvậ
(3). Bhailkhvậ
(4). Lapu
(5). Purậtvậ

(1). Gvagahkvậ is the curvilinear wings of wood that extend from the frame half-way up its height on either side of the opening to penetrate the brick wall between the upright of the portal frame and the projecting lintel. These Curvilinear outlines of the wings are not structurally necessary, nor do they seem to be the natural outgrowth of the basic door frame. They are not found on domestic or palace buildings and even many temples, especially shrines of Buddhist orientation. These wings are roughly quadrant-shaped curved architectural elements based on two concentric circles. The outer section of this wing starts from the base of portal frame of door frame. It is a concave curve turning inward about half way up the bracket circumscribing a small sac-like bulge and then running in a convex curve as far as the lower edge of the lintel end. In the lower part of the wing there is makara (water beast) with its mouth wide open. Tails of makara ends in flamboyant curls of vegetation that fill large parts of wing. From the mouth of this water beast emerges the

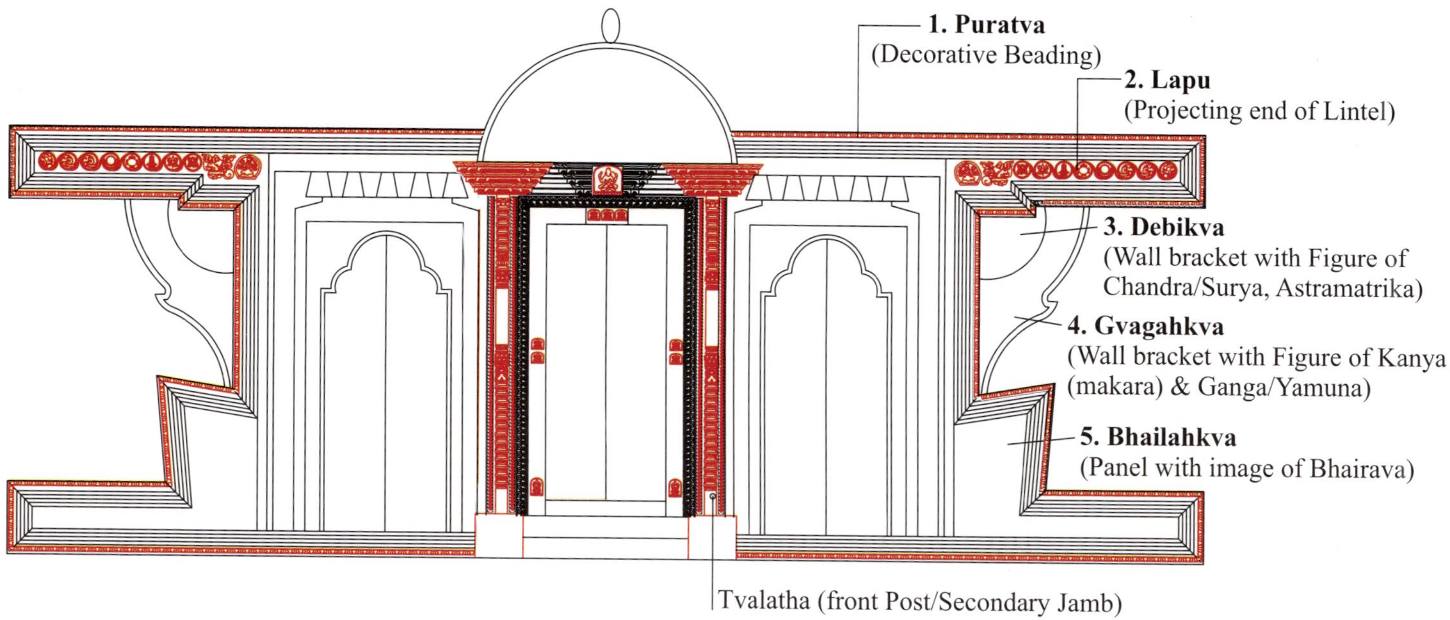

Figure 25. *Typical Elevation of Door*

figure of deities, especially goddesses. These goddesses are river goddesses Ganga in the left and Yamuna in the right symbolizing the river by which man is cleansed of all impurities of his human state. Their bodies are twisted unnaturally in many representations.

Plate IX B. *Detail of Upper Door Wing (Gvagậhkvậ) Pachali Mahadeva Temple*

(2). Debikvậ is part of the inner curvilinear wing with quarter round panels next to images of river goddesses. In this panel there are the images of Chandra on the left and Surya on the right flanking the main door.

(3). Bhailkhvậ is a panel above the sill of the door and at the bottom of door frames and have figure of guardian. These figures often occupy their own rectilinear frame. They function on behalf of the deity enshrined in the Garbha Girha. They often take on the terrific form of the main gods like Mahankala who guards the shrines of his master Shiva. As dwarpala or guardian demi-gods they hold in their hands weapons that are recognizable as belonging to the deity or deties.

Plate IX C. *Detail of Lower Door Wing (Bhailahkvậ) Pachali Mahadeva Temple, Kathmandu*

(4). Lapu is the projecting Lintel of door frame which is another characteristic feature of wooden door. These projections act as additional elements bearing the load of the massive entablature above. These frames are joined together around the edge of the frame before the face of the brick wall. These projections bear quite range of motifs which can be grouped into four categories, namely:

(i) Religious.
(ii) Floral or Geometrical
(iii) Animal
(iv) Combined.

In the first category of religious motifs, which contains eight auspicious symbols (astamangalas), four are placed on either side with the moon to the left and the sun to the right. The eight auspicious symbols are lotus, umbrella, holy water jar, endless knot, conch shell, flag, wheel, and a pair of fish. The moon is shown seated with a lotus flower on either side in a chariot driven by fourteen geese, while the sun is shown riding a chariot drawn by seven or nine horses symbolizing the seven days in a week or the nine planets. Besides eight auspicious symbols, several other mythological motifs are also carved on the lintel projections. Figures of Shiva, Vaisnava, tantric and Buddhist affinities are all incorporated in the decorative scheme.

In the second category of floral motifs, floral like full-blown lotus, the vine and spray are quite common.

In the third category of animal motifs, a number of animals, winged dragons, crocodiles, deer, elephants, doves, peacocks and swans are often found.

In the fourth category of combined motifs, all the above motifs are often combined like floral motif combined with endless knot of religious motif. Dragon (Malah) and creeper (Gasi) pattern predominate other motifs mentioned above but there are however, no restrictions to the inventiveness of the craftsman.

(5). Puratvậ is the outer decorative beading around the whole frame. Decorative motifs such as geometric borders or floral designs are more typical in this frame.

Within the door frame there is a free standing post called Tvalatha. These posts are richly decorated with kalasa (ritual pot) design in the middle. These posts are placed between the secondary lintel and the secondary sill. These posts are multiplied to add formative character of a door. Most common design motifs in these posts are egg pattern, lotus leaves and geometric patterns.

Door lintels on top of the door frame typically depict a trio of gods or trimurti. The lower part of lintel of the door is usually a trapezoidal form of dentils. The dentil pattern which is uneven in number is understood as an auspicious symbol. The symmetrical trapezoid has embedded decorations.

The square temples of bigger size without surrounding colonnades have large size doors with three openings on their four sides. The middle opening has a straight or arched lintel, whereas the others have cusped arches. Secondary lintels or tympanums may emphasize the middle opening.

The door leaves are plain, grilled or decorated with various motifs. In the oldest temples of Kathmandu, Patan and Bhaktapur, grilled door leaves are found associated with the main shrines door.

Manakamana temple in Kathmandu, though a temple of minor importance and no fame, has some marvellous door carvings. It is rarer that bronze plating is applied to doors or doorframes, Chagu Narayana, Bajra Yogni of Sankhu and Kathmandu's Taleju shrine being among the exceptions in this respect since both beautifully utilize thin overlays of metal sheeting on door areas.

Chapter 10

Column (Tha)

Columns in Nepalese temples are structural members to transfer load from upper portion of temple to its foundation. Columns in temples are generally square /rectangular in shape, and are oversized due to carved portions. Besides its structural function it is also decorative part of temple. Usually the columns are made out of wood and used in place of wall to create open space. In temples, use of columns provides circumambulatory space outside Garbha Girha.

Column can be divided into three parts, namely: (i) Wooden Bracket (meth), (ii) Wooden Post (Tha), (iii) Wooden threshold (lakashin) and stone base (e-lohan).

Wooden bracket is a separate piece of wood connected to the column with the help of wooden peg of wooden post. Wooden bracket transfers the load from the lintel and beams on to the post supported by the wooden threshold. The Meth has rectangular central part with bracket on both sides. Wooden peg extends from the central portion of the post passes through the bracket into the beam and holds the three structural elements in position. The decorative motifs on such brackets and capitals are manifold, but may be classified broadly as:

a. Floral motif

b. Animal motifs like that of dragon, elephant and deer etc.

c. Mythological scenes connected with Krishna legend and Rama legends.

d. The Buddhist, Shiva, Vaisnava, and Tantric Deties.

e. Secular motifs like hunting scene, amorous couples.

Plate X A. *View of Columns of Pachali Mahadeva Temple Kathmandu*

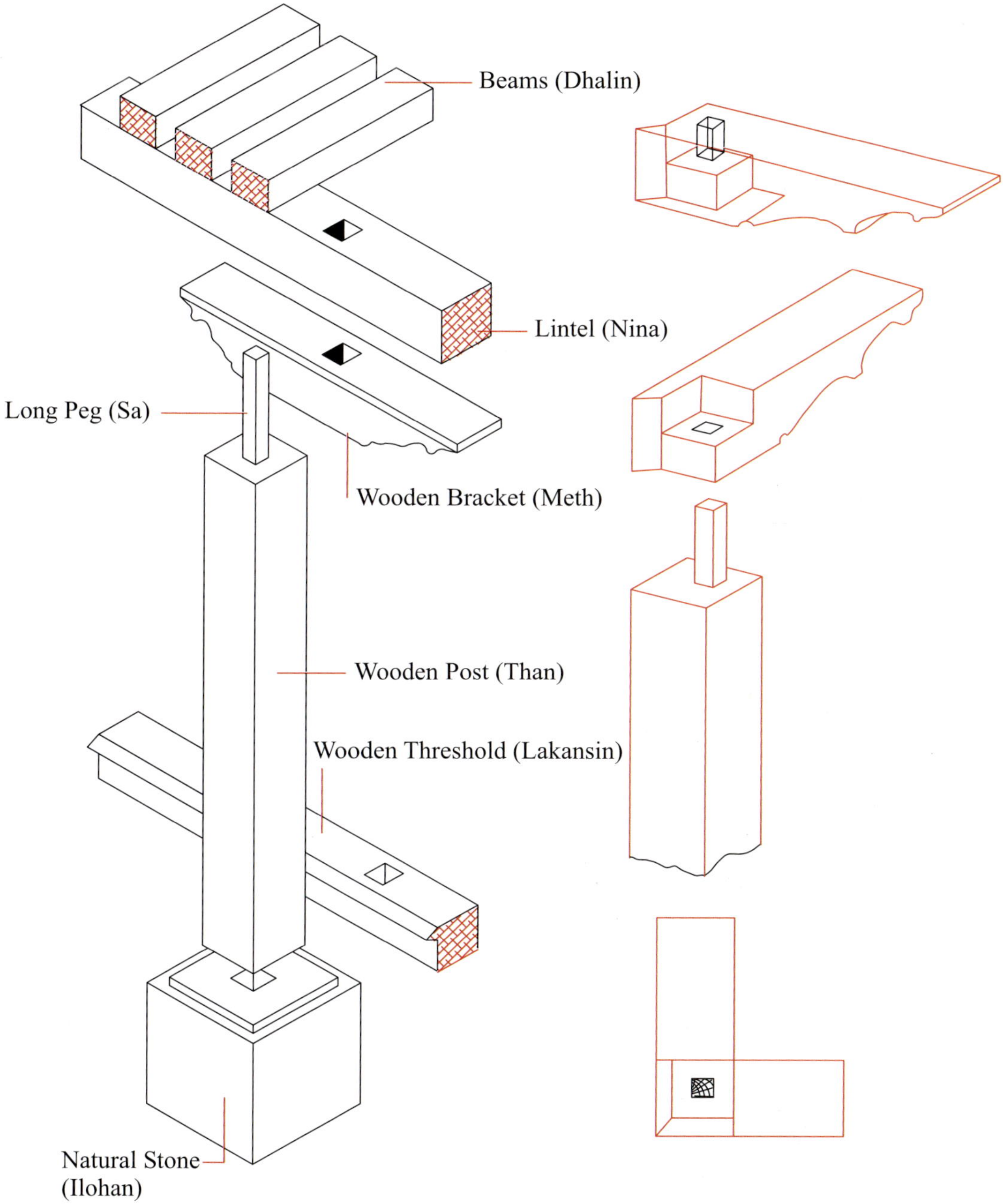

Figure 26. *Assemble Details of Column at Centre & Corner*

On the whole, the brackets are free from the erotic scenes. The central panel coming on the top of column and at the centre of the byways projections of brackets is either blank or equipped with the carving of deities and floral pattern.

Columns are usually even in number creating odd number of bays in between them. Twin columns are also used to support the load of thick walls. The height to width ratio of column located in ground floor temple varies from 1:6 to 1:7. This ratio of height to width is less than Greek column having ratio of 1:7 to 1:10.

Columns of the temple can be classified into two types,

(a). Those with square shaft and b). those with cylindrical shaft

In the case of column with square shaft, either the lower portion is square and plain or more than half of the shaft is square with the edges having scroll design. Except these variations, the decoration consists of foliage, mouldings, cushions, beadings, loops, florals

Plate X B. *Upper Column Detail Of Pachali Mahadava Temple, Kathmandu*

and amlakas, naga-pasa, garuda, purna-kalasa and panels depicting seated or standing gods and goddesses, Shiva-linga and astamangala medallions. In several cases the entire height of a column is heavily ornamented right from the base.

The cylindrical shaft is rarely invariably decorated with floral design, scale, and circle diapers.

Columns mostly found in temples are carved to the full length except a small lower portion at the base. The carvings in the column have the same god or related to the god inside the Garbhagriha in different tantric pose. The carvings of gods occurs maximum at two levels, Upper and lower level in one face of column. These columns have purna kalasha near the base since they usually surround a shrine.

According to Ishwaranand, different parts of column are Chakula, Guti, Nahagvah and Kalas.

Plate X C. *Lower Column Detail of Pachali Mahadava Temple, Kathmandu*

Chakula is a pattern of circular rings which occurs at different positions in column. Among these one lies just below meth, receives the load from the meth and transfers it to the pillar.

Guti is stepped design on column with different motifs.

Naghgvah is intermediate band of wood between two motifs.

Kalas is a ritual pot

The carvings of columns in temples mostly have the following motifs. These motifs are shown in figure 27 and figure 28.

Paleha (lotus leaf) is a prominent floral pattern -- which occurs frequently.

Keshar (row of androecia) -- occur maximum two times at different positions.

Memikha (row of buffalo eyes) -- occurs only once at mid portion

Khosingo (row of walnuts) -- occurs only once at upper portion.

Palego row of relatively small spheres -- generally one at lower portion.

Nago a flattened sphere, symbolizing a drop of water -- occurs mostly above and below memikha.

Kalash (ritual pot) -- generally found in lower portion of pillars at temples,

Jhallar-(lace) -- mostly found twice at upper and lower portion.

Dyatwa (deity portion) -- occurs twice at maximum at the upper and lower portions.

Gasi (flower leaves).

Eacth motif on the column has its own philosophical and cultural importance. These carved columns not only enhance the beauty of temple but also bear high cultural and social value.

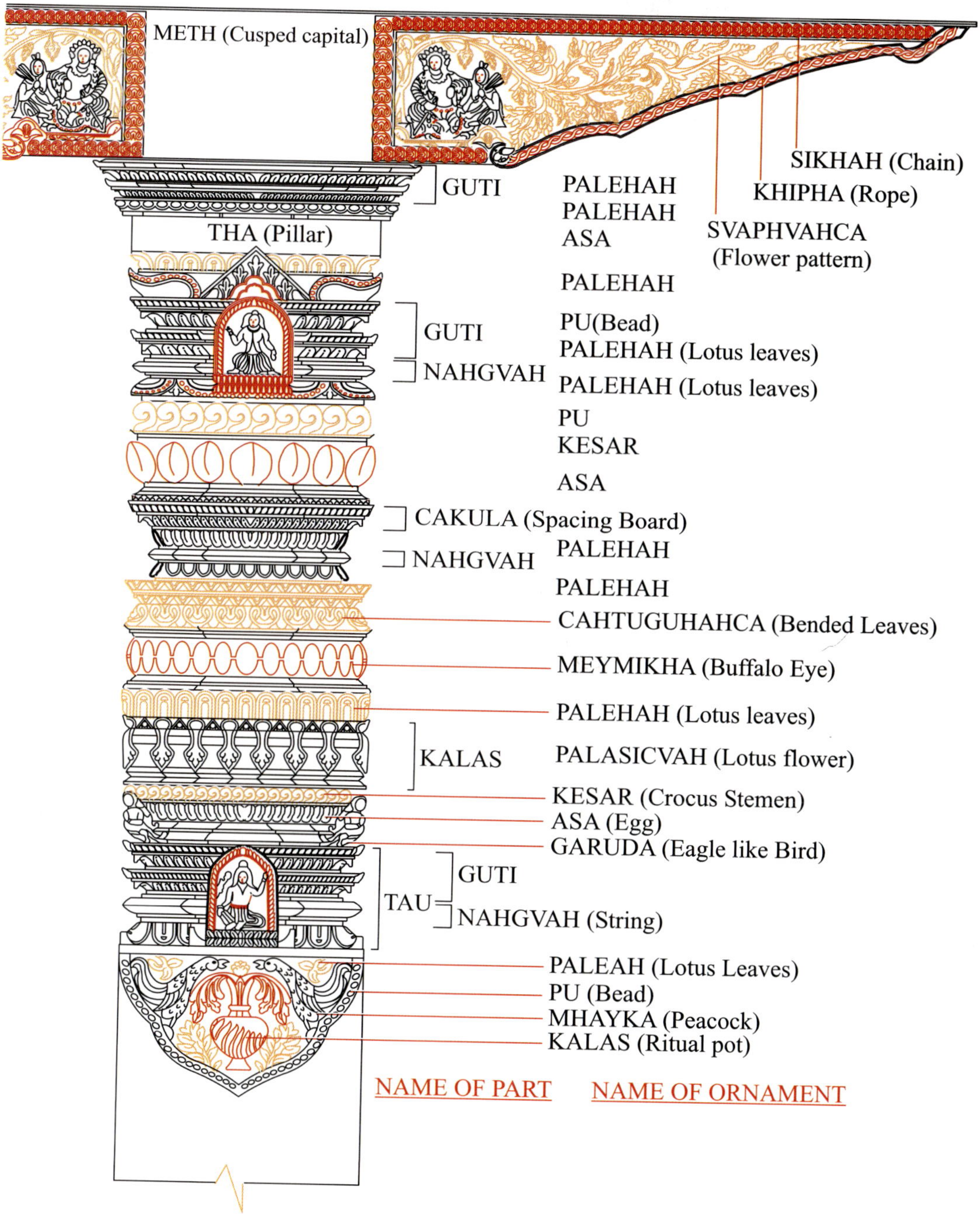

Figure 27. *Elevation of Column Kathmandu: Darbar - Lvahacuka Peacocks (Mhaykhs) in a cusped Madallion. (I. Shresthcharya)*

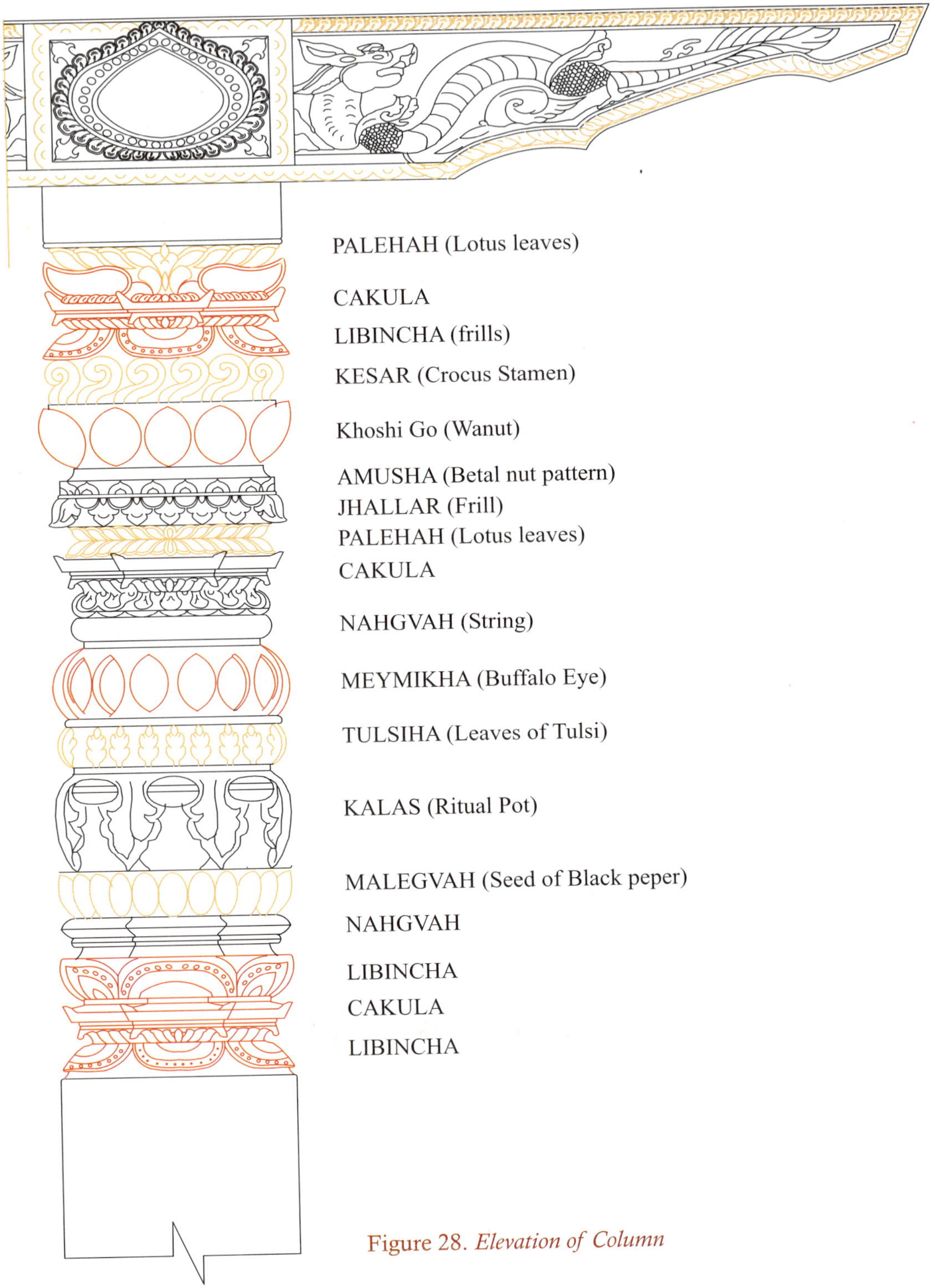

Figure 28. *Elevation of Column*

Each face of column can be divided into divisions of the square equivalent to the width of column. Small division of carving fit into specific divisions of the squares.

Plate X D. *View of Column of Pachali Mahadeva Temple Kathmandu*

Chapter 11

Plinth

The plinth is the base of temple which sets it apart from its immediate environment. The plinth is more than a pedestal having a stepped base of two or more levels. It lifts the shrine above the wet and muddy street level or damp court yard and separates it to some extent from its surroundings and activities of the people. A stepped plinth is a striking architectural feature for the aggrandizement of temple. Above all, the plinth of the free standing temple of square plan reflects its derivation from the mandala, the prime factor governing its form. In relation to the total scheme of sacred design, it is the boundary of the temple's internal universe.

The visible portion of the plinth is made of brick or stone, with the top of each step often paved with stone. In most cases stone is used as a kind of reinforced trim on the plinth and it is never a major structural part of the temple. Plinth being the important part of the temple, it is the setting for numerous symbolic, decorative and practical objects of essential association with the holy structure.

The plinth is marked at the entrance side of the temple by stone or brick steps bound by low balustrades or borders that separate the stairway from the high platforms of the base. Stone lions and other guardian beasts, minor deities and semi-miraculous human figures are usually mounted beside the stairs. Lions are the most common guardians and they are often vividly colourful, as at Svata Kali in Katmandu. Their open mouth with sharp teeth, massive frowning brows and glaring eyes, show their fierceness. The guardians of Jagatnarayan temple in Patan stand with weapons in hand at the top of the plinth, as do most such minor deities. Large-scale guardians are always of stone and face outward from the temple towards the visitors. In Nyatapola temple animals and figures are mounted hierarchically according to their relative physical power or religious power besides its stairway. These figures are chosen for their ability to guard the temple and its approaches from the evil impulses of both spirits and men.

Plate XI A. *Multi Level Plinth of Maju Temple, Kathmandu*

Plate XI B. *Guardians in Multi Level Plinth of Nyatapole Temple, Bhaktapure*

Early Malla period temples usually have one or two level of plinth like in temples of Changu Narayan, Indraswore Mahadev of Panauti, Pashupatnath and Kumbheswore temple[1] of Patan. Late Malla Period temples have high stepped multi-level plinth. The multi-stage plinth is found in the twelve-stage plinth of Taleju temple of Kathmandu, the highest plinth in Nepal and Maju temple in Basantapur with high stepped plinth of nine levels. The Taleju and Maju temple were built in 1584 A.D and 1690 A.D. respectively and the Nyatapole Temple of Taumadhi square in Bhaktapue built in 1702 A.D. are excellent examples of such temples. The structure of these multi-stepped plinths is yet unknown. Whether the plinth is raised in several stages or is merely a symbolic square lying flushed with the pavement of the brick courtyard, it is an essential part of the total plan. Temples having five tiered roofs like Nytapola have high plinth of five levels whereas Kumbhaswore which also has a five tiered roof has a plinth

Plate XI C. *Secondary Shrines in Plinth of Tripuraswore Mahadeva Temple*

of one level. The relationship between the number of plinth and the number of roofs is yet to be studied.

If the plinth has several platforms of large size then secondary shrines are also placed. Taleju temple with twelve-stepped plinth has many small traditional style shrines containing the panchayana gods and the guardians of the eight directions (Astadikpals). The twelve-stepped plinth is divided into three horizontal levels, viz. a high, three-stepped lower section having a broad terrace lined with twelve secondary shrines: a further three stepped plinth with four secondary shrines at four corner of its terrace, which is enclosed by a wall. From this terrace a third, very steep, three-stepped base rises which serves as platform for the main temple.

Tripureswore Mahadev temple also has secondary shrines at its four corners at second level of the plinth. The secondary shrines in four corners of temple are in the southeast a Surya, in the southwest a Ganesh, in the North West a Bhagavati and in the north east a Satya Narayana. The plan of this temple is based on the concept of the Panchayan, whereby Shiva is surrounded by four demigods. The main Mahadeva temple is set on the fourth level of the diminishing plinth.

The plinths of some temple have bricks with decorative mouldings. The temple with decorative bricks in plinth is found in Mahadev temple at Pachali. It has several rows of moulded bricks on each of its foundation steps. A line of three-dimensional lotus flowers is the most delicate motif, while other rows of bricks present borders of entwined snakes and various medallions and roundels. At the upper four corners of the three stages of the plinth, winged lions stand below each column to punctuate the decorative field of the brick wall. The lowest level of bricks forms a bevel at the base of each step of the plinth, meeting the stones of the courtyard at the bottom level of the base.

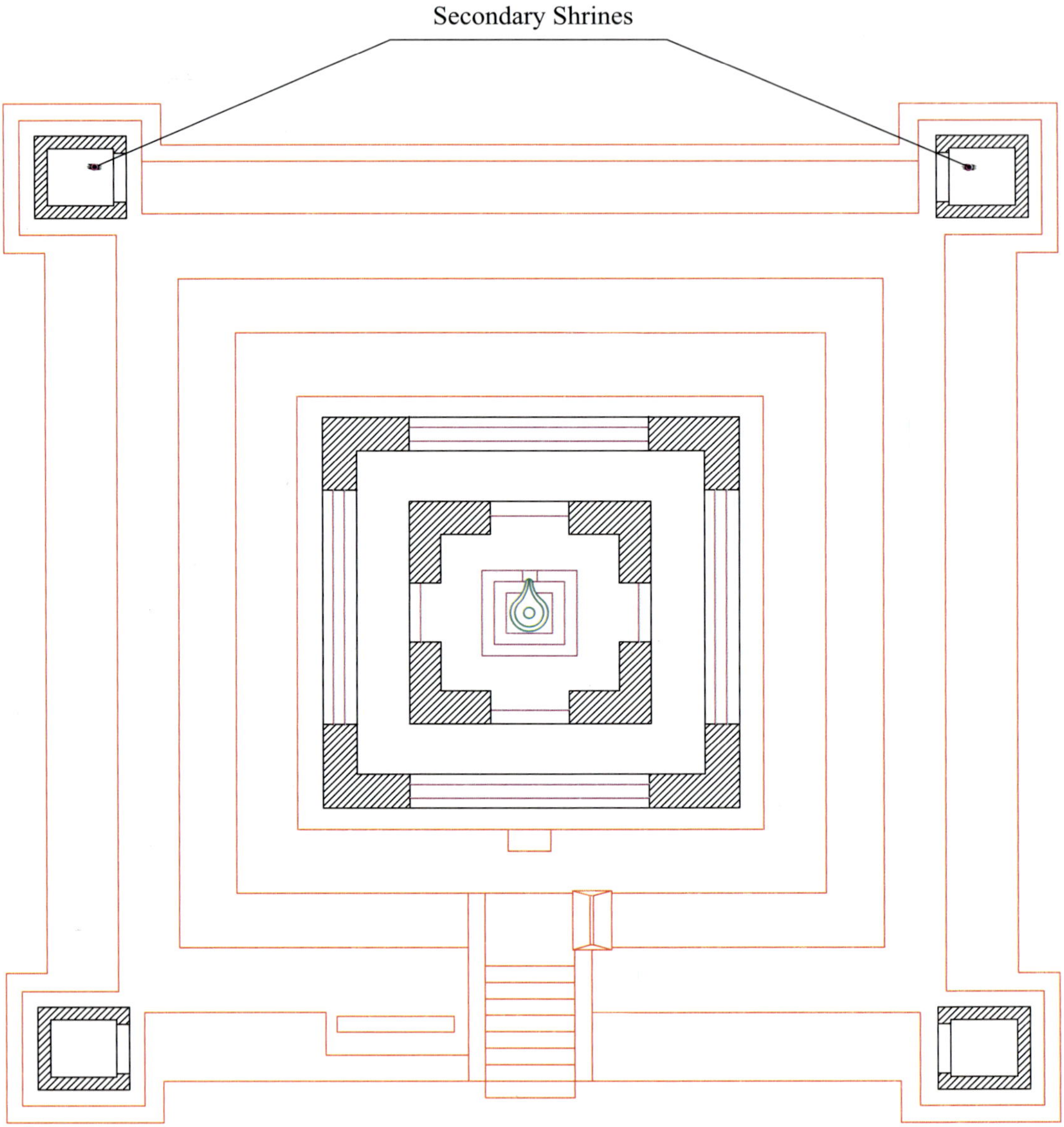

Figure 29. *Plan of Plinth with Secondary Shrines at Tripuraswore Mahadev Temple, Kathmandu*

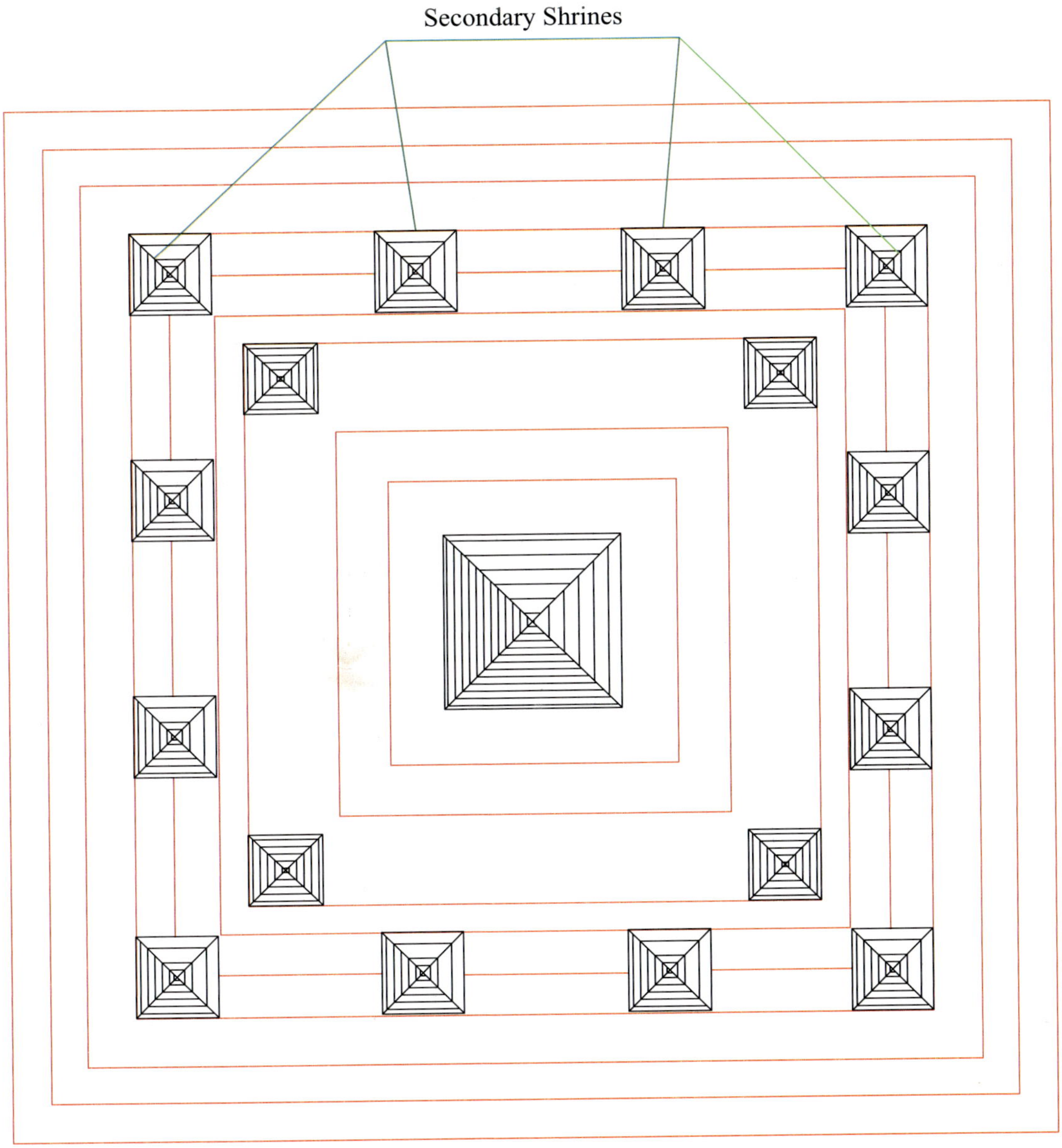

Figure 30. *Plan of Plinth with Several Plateform at Talaju Temple, Kathmandu*

Plate XI D. *Secondary Shrines in Plinth of Talaju Temple, Kathmandu*

Notes

1. Kumbheswore temple This temple is composed of five storey above two level plinth. The four lower roofs of the temple are of tile and uppermost roof is of gilt copper. The sacred image of the temple is a linga about 3' high mounted with four faces of Siva.It is located in Patan.

Appendices

These tables give an idea about the symbols, vehicles, number of hands and faces of various gods and goddess to aid the readers in their identification.

Appendix 1. Key to the identification of major gods and goddesses (R.S.Gupte)

God/godesses	Symbol	Vehicle	Hands	Faces	Misc.
1. Bramha	Rosary,vase,ladle,book	goose	Four	Four, actually three seen	Generally shown with short pointed bear
2. Vishnu	Mace, lotus,counch, wheel	Eagle (Garuda)	Four	one	Sometimes wears flower garland as the sacred thread
3. Shiva	Trident,wheel,battle axe,club, often a deer in hand	bull	Two, four	one	Often crescent and serpend in the hair & third eye on forehead
4. Mahesa-Murti	Four right hand-sula, battle axe, thunder bolt & sword Four left hand- shield, goad, noose & shield	ten	Five, only four visible		
5. Dakshina-murti-Shiva	Right hand- one in Janana mudra & one carriesa rosary Left hand- boon giving pose& fire snake or lotus		Four		Seated with one leg pendant
6. Natraja -Shiva	R.H- protection pose & drum L.H-in Gajahasta & fire	Stand on dwarf apsara, left leg lifted, turned towards right leg & kept across it.	Four	one	

God/godesses	Symbol	Vehicle	Hands	Faces	Misc.
7. Karttikeya	Two hands in protection & boon giving poses, other carrying thun derbolt, shield, spear & sword	Peacock	Six	Two or six	Sometimes with four faces. The peacock identifies him from Bramha. Sometimes with one head & four head but without deer or serpents.
8. Ganesh	Elephant tooth, goad, laddu, noose	Rat	Four	one	
9. Virabhadra	Protection pose, tridentmace, mace & boon giving pose.	Bull	Four	one	
10. Sheshasahi-vishnu	Conch, wheel, one hand on the head of serpent shesha & one on knee.	Serpent sheshu	Four		One foot held by consort Sri on her lap: Bramha on lotus springing out of his navel. Demons Madhu & Kaitabha near stalk of lotus
11. Lakshmi-	Lotus, conch, wheel, fourth hand embraces Lakshmi	Eagle (Garuda)	Four		Four sitting posture
12. Rama	Bow & arrow	–	Two		Accompanied by Sita, Lakshmana, Bharata & Shatrughna
13. Krishna	R.H- Curved Stick L.H -lifted up & bent at elbow		Two		Rukmini on right Styabhama on left
14. Brahmani	Rosary, ladle, vase, vase	Goose	Four	Four	
15. Mahesvari	Bow arrow, wheel, bow	Bull	Four or Six		
16. Kumari	Spear in both hands	peacock	Two ,four twelve		
17. Vaishnavi	Wheel,mace, conch, lotus	Bull	Four or six		
18. Varahi	Staff, conch, wheel,mace	Bull	?	Boar face	
19. Indrani	Thunderbolts in both hands	Elephant	Four		
20. Chamunda	Javelin, Katri,Skull cup, steel staff with sharp point		Four or ten		
21. Parvati	Rosary, Siva, Ganapati, vase		Four		
22. Gauri	Sula & mirror		Two		

God/godesses	Symbol	Vehicle	Hands	Faces	Misc.
23. Mahalakshmi	Mahalunga,maceshield, bowl of leaves		Four		
24. Sarasvati	Bow,mace,noose,lute, wheel,conch,pestle, goad, sometimes rosary	peacock		Four or eight	
25. Indra	Thundrbolt, lotus	Elephant Airavati		Two or Four	
26. Agni	Rosary,Vase	Goat		Two or Four	
27. Yama	Staff, noose	Buffalo		Two or Four	
28. Nirruti	Sword,shield, Katri	Man, ass or Camel		Two or Four	
29. Varuna	Noose ,Lotus	Crocodile		Two or Four	
30. Vayu	Boon giving & Banner	Stag		Two or Four	
31. Isana	Trident & Boon Giving	White bull		Two or Four	
32. Kubera	Mace & Boon giving	Man, Goat or horse		Two or Four	
33. Surya	Lotus in each of two hands	One wheel chariot driven by seven horses		Two	Danda & pingala on two sides carrying sward and shield

Appendix 2. Key to the identification of Planets (Grahas). (R.S.Gupte)

Planets	Symbole	Vehicle	Hands	Misc.
1. Sun (Surya)	Lotus in each of two hands	One wheeled chariot driven by 7 horses or one horse with 7 heads	Two	Kirita crown: danda & Pingala on two sides carrying shield & sword. A writer holding a pen: sometimes wives Rajani & Nikshubha holding fly whisks.
2. Moon (Chandra)	Mace & varda pose or vase & rosary or	Chariot driven by 10 horses	Two	Rohini or righ, Kanti & Shobha, wives on two sides (sometimes)
3. Mars (Mangala)	Vara, Javelin, mace or Kjavelin & rosary, or staff & vase or Shakti Javelin, mace ritual wand	Goat	Two or four	
4. Mercury (Rudha)	Vara, sword shield, mace, or bow & rosary or yoga mudra	Lion	Two or four	Lion or chariot driven by 4 horses
5. Jupiter (Brihspati)	Vara, rosary vase, staff or book & rosary or vase & rosary	Golden chariot driven by 8 horses	Two ro four	
6. Venus (Sukra)	Vara, rosary vase, staff or vase & rosary	Chariot driven by 8 or 10 horses	Two or four	
7. Saturn(Sani)	Vara, arrow, bow, Javelin or staff & varaor Staff & vase, staff & rosary	Vulture, he-buffalo, chariot driven by 8 vultures	Two or four	
8. Rahu	Vara, sword,shield, javelionanjali mudra		Two	Carved like half moon, Ugly faced tiger mouth
9. Ketu	Vara & mace or sword & lamp	Vulture	Four	Like serpent -tail ugly face

Appendix 3. Key to the identification of Vishnu Incarnations. (R.S.Gupte)

Incarnations	Symbols	Hands	Objects in Hand	Misc.	Variations
1. Nara-Narayana	Conch, wheel, lotus, rosary	Two or four	Left hand carry conch and wheel. Right hands hold Mahapadma or mace and lotus(?) Narayana (CC)	Sri holdingl flute on left. Musti holding lotus on right	*Two-handed*: nara two hands carrying rosary: Narayana-four hands carrying rosary, Chariot vehicle (VID)
2. Narasimha	Wheel, mace, conch, lotus	Two four, six or eight	Wheel, lotus, mace and conch (AC)	Ferocious countenance	1. 4-*handed*: wheel, mace, two hands tearing off entrails. Open- mouthed (AGP) 2. 6-*handed*: conch and lotus, two tearing entrails of Hiranyakasya, two on maces, Mane of flames (VID) 3. 8-*handed*:1&8, tearing entrails of Hiranyakasya; 4&5<holding garland of entrails; 2&3, wheel and lotus; 6&7, mace and conch(AC)
3. Parasurama	Battle-axe	Two or four	Sword, battle- -axe, bow ,arrow	Jata crown	1. 1&4 Bow and Arrow, 2&3 sword and battle-axe(AGP) 2. Conch, wheel and mace(SS)
4. Balarama	Plough, pestle	Two or four	Plough, pestle, mace, conch	------	1. *two handed*: mace and plough(AGP) 2. *four handed*: wheel pestle, plough,conch(AGP) 3. *two handed*: plough and pestle(RM and VID) 4. *two handed*: plough and pestle(SS) or plough and wine-flask(ST) 5. *Four handed*: wheel and pestle(SS)
5.Buddha	Boon-giving protection poses or in dhyana	Two	Boon-giving protection poses(AGP)	Long ears, deer-skin on shoulder	In dhyana pose, red garments, deer skin on shoulders(RM & VID)
6. Matsya	–	–	Conch wheel boon giving and protection poses	Lower half fish: upper half, four- -handed Vishnu, Kirita crown	

Incarnations	Symbols	Hands	Objects in Hand	Misc.	Variations
7. Kurma	–	–	Conch and wheel varaha abhaya poses	lower half, tortoise; upper half, four- handed Vishnu	
8. Rama	Bow and arrow	Two or four four	Bow and arrow (AC)		1.*two handed*: bow and arrow arrow(AC)2.*four handed*: bow arrow conch 3. Wears a kirita crown *Companions*: Sita stands on his right, L.h.- blue lotus, R.h.- hangs loose on right. Laksmana stands of left side of Rama. Holds bow and arrow. Hanumana, Monkey-god, stands in front, on Rama's right. Two hands R.h.- on mouth, L.h.- hangs loose on left *Bharata and Shatraguna* Rama's brothers. Hold bows and arrows Rama seated in virasana
9. Varadaraja	Wheel and conch in upper two hands: one hand in varada, other on waist- lower than hands	Four		If lower hand rests on mace, he Varadaraja	
10. Mohini		Vase of nectar		Beautiful young lady wearing colourful garments. Decorated with ornaments. Carrying a vase of nectar in hand	

Appendix 4. Typical Hand poses (mudras):

JNAN MUDRA. Indicates wisdom. Tips of thumb and forefinger or second finger jointed to form a circle. Hand is held at centre of breast, palm outward, with rest of fingers pointing upward. Typical of Manjusri, of Shiva in his teaching role and of Sakyamuni.

VARDHA MUDRA. Bestowing blessing. Hand points down, palm out with fingers extended. Typical of Buddha Ratna sambhavan avalokitesvaren Sakyamuni.

DHARMA CHAKRA MUDRA. Turning the wheel of the doctrine. Right hand held outwards in front of breast, tip of first finger touching tip of thumb. The left hand is held palm inwards a little beyond the right. The tips of thumb and forefingers of the right hand touch the end of one of the fingers of the left. Typical of Buddha Maitreya and Sakyamuni.

TARFANI MUDRA. Threatening. Hand up, palm out; first finger pointing up, others closed. Typical of Shiva.

ABHAYA MUDRA. Dauntlessness. Hand upward, turned toward the visitor with fingers and thumb raised upward. Typical of Amoghasiddhi. (North)

EARTH WITNESS. Hand pointing towards the earth palm inwards, fingers extended. Typical of Akshobhy (East) and of Sakyamuni.

MEDITATION. Hands on lap, one on top of the other, palm upwards. Typical of Amitabha(West) and of Sakyamuni.

Appendix 5. Manuscripts

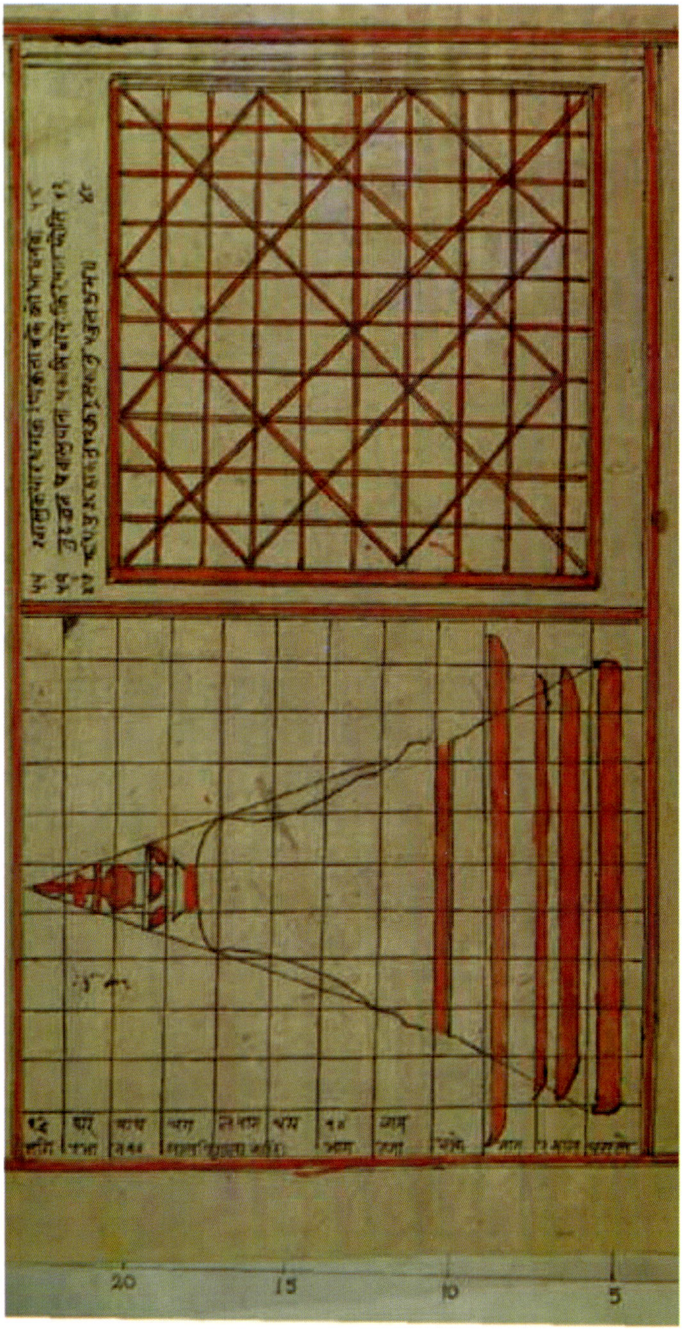

Palte XII A. *Manuscript of Gajure Detail of Kankeswore Temple*

(Source: Asha Sapi Kuthi)

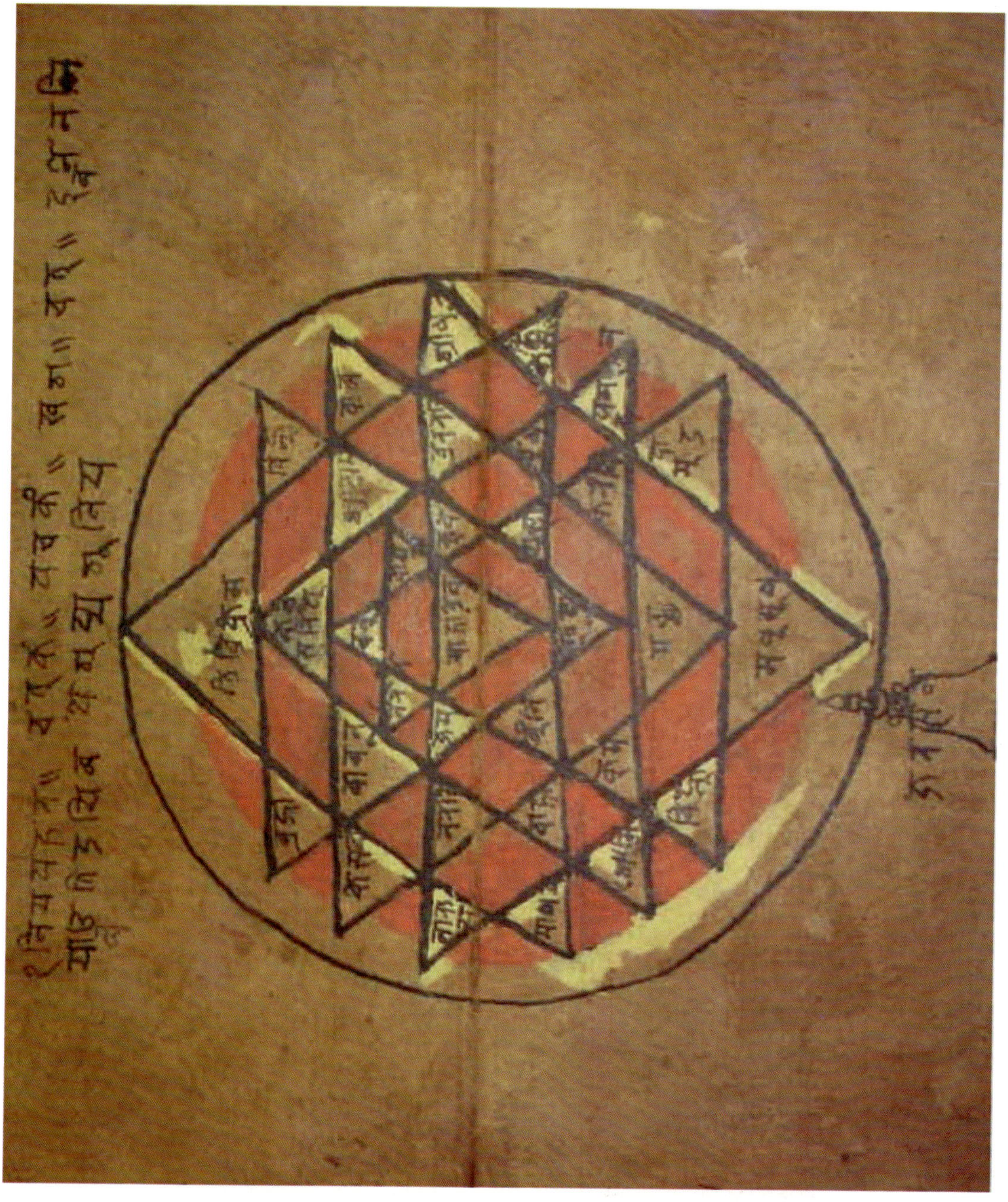

Palte XII B. *Manuscript of Struts in Srianti for Narayan Temple*

(Source: Keshor Library)

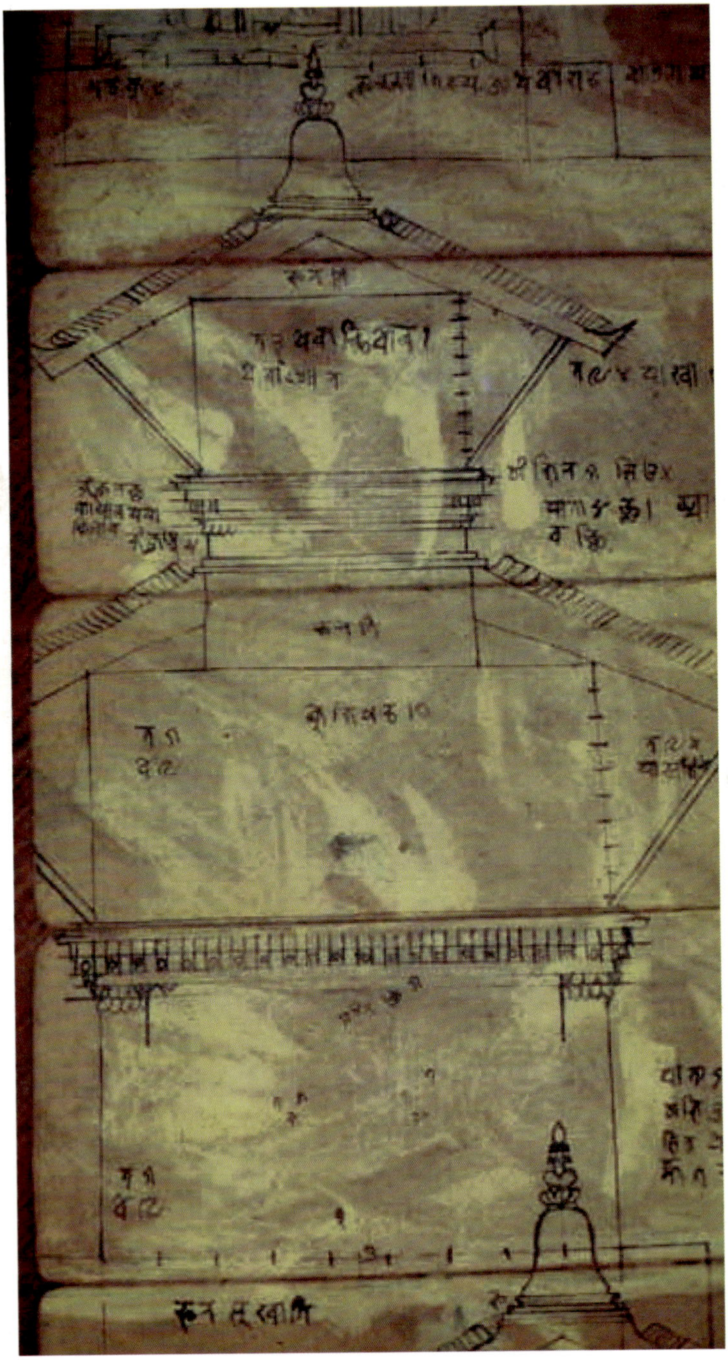

Palte XII C. *Manuscript of Narayan Temple*

(Source: Keshor Library)

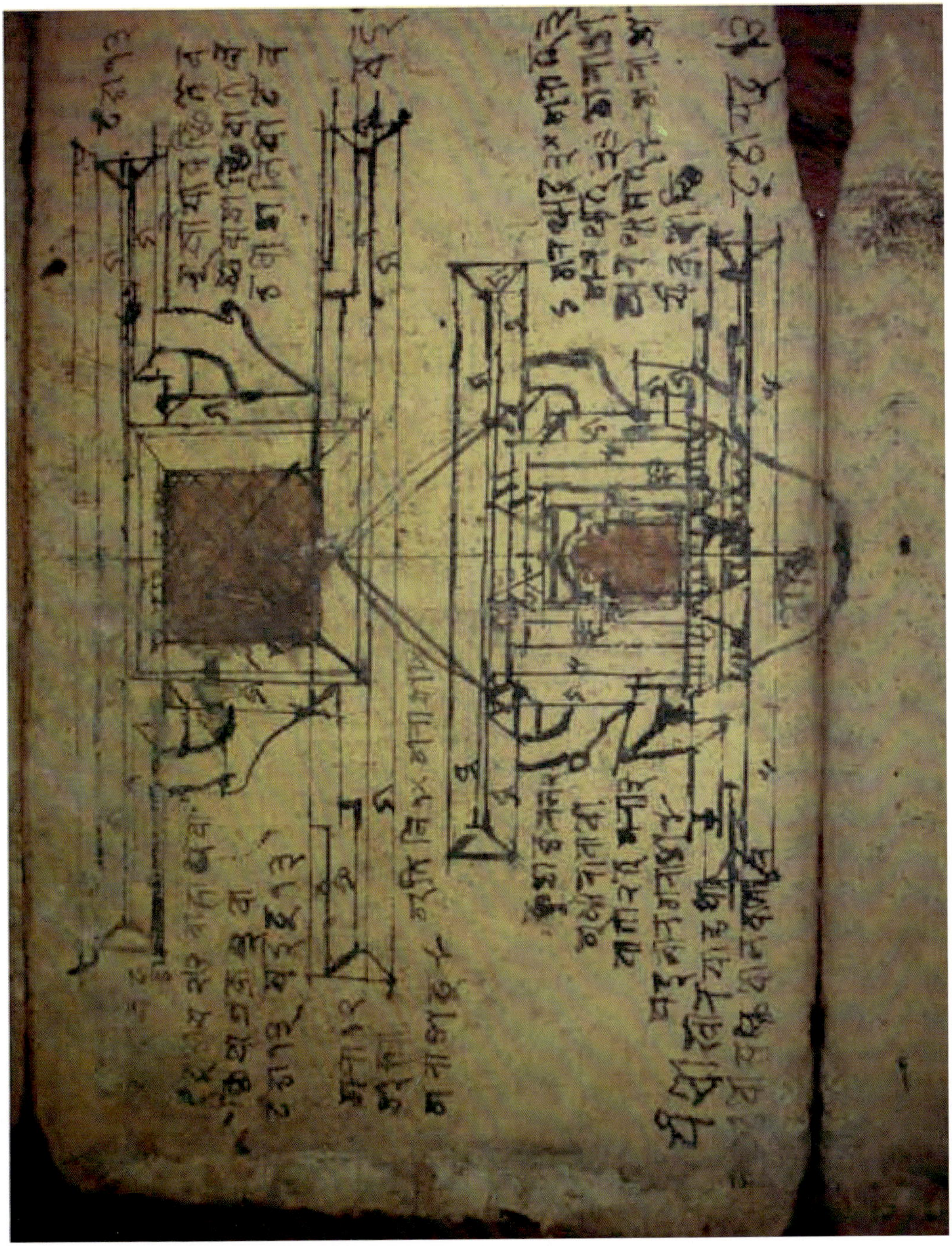

Palte XII D. *Manuscript of Window Detail*

(Source: Keshor Library)

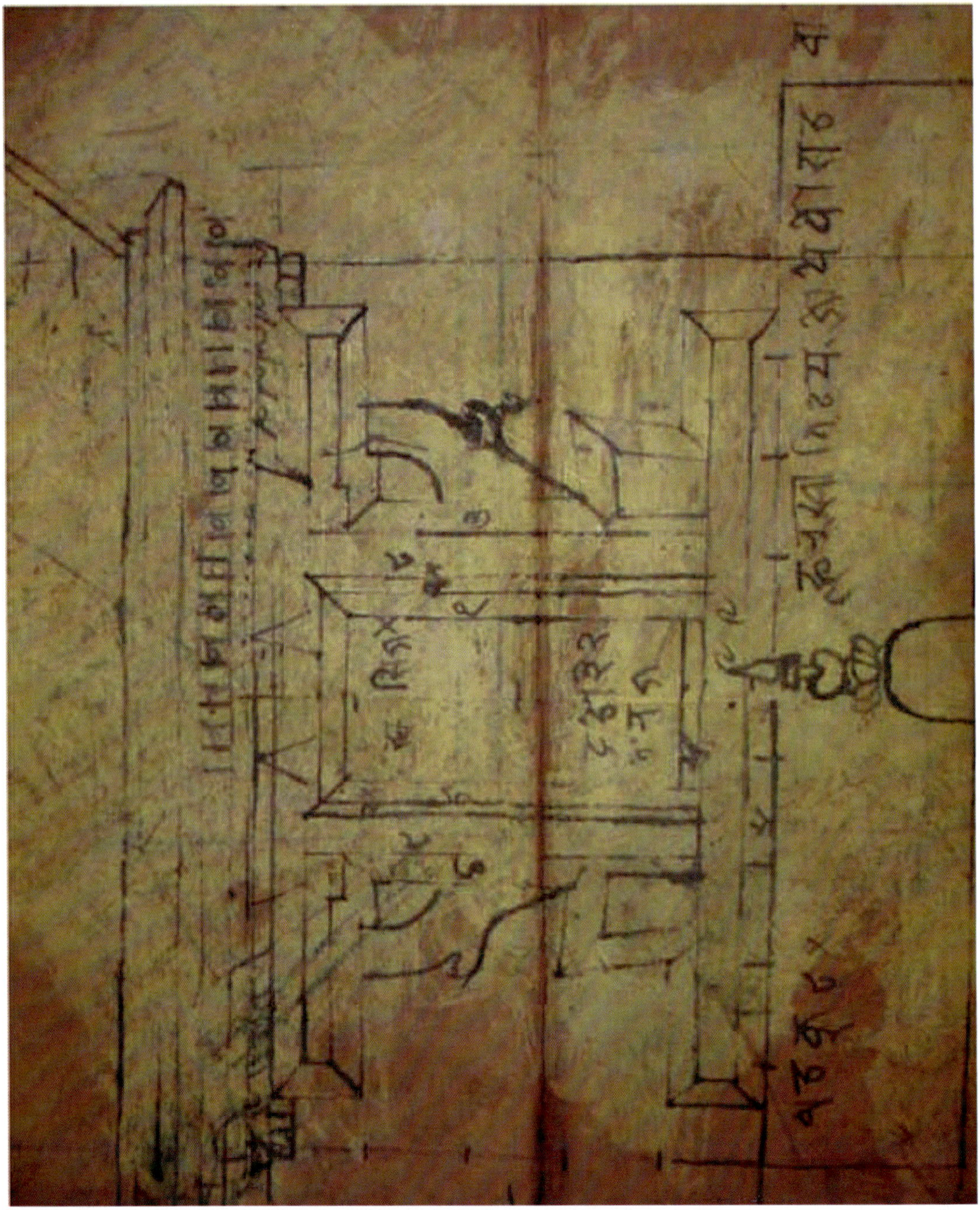

Palte XII E. *Manuscript of Door Detail*

(Source: Keshor Library)

Appendix 6. Patterns of Decoration

NEWARI	ENGLISH	ILLUSTRATION	OCCURRENCE
Javala Jvah Jvalca (PA) Jhallar Jhyahkapah	Water/Wave Frill Frill (Lit window curtain, jhallar)		Cornice, String Course, Secondary Sill
Tika	Beehive (Hanche)	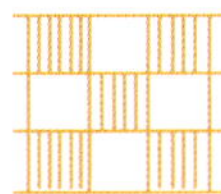	Secondary Jamb
Tichu Tusipu	Shrew cucumber seed	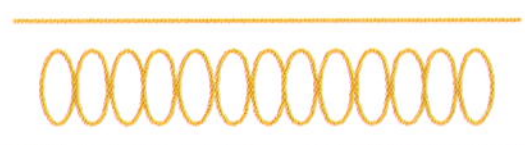	Projecting ends of lintel and sill **Pillar**, Capital, Window/ Door Frame
Desiphvah Desisva Dvaphvasva	Foreign Flower Flower		**Pillar,** Cornice (Typical 19th century design)
Naga Nagvah	Snake (1) Stylized Snake (2)	 	Pillar Window/Colour Frame, String Course
Nagkanya Nagapas Nagabeli	Female Snake Twisted Snake Zigzag	 	Window/Door Frame, String Course
Nhayca	Nose		Cornice, Lintel
Palasicvah	Lotus leaf		Pillar
Palepu Palesva	Lotus Seed Lotus Flower		Window/Door Frame

NEWARI	ENGLISH	ILLUSTRATION	OCCURRENCE
Palehah	Lotus Leaf		Pillar, Window/Door Frame, String Course
Payahphvah	Flower in Block		Pillar
Pu	Bead	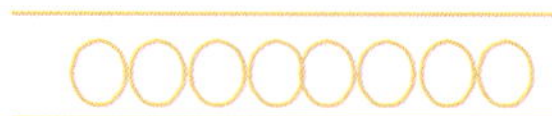	Pillar, Capital, Window Door Frame, String Course
Phlikula Phvsikva	Mythical Animal (Horse) Tooth (Litjackfruit)		Wall bracket of window Lintel
Baithaca	Fish Hook	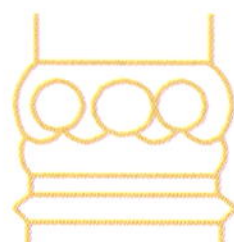	Pillar
Bajramalah Baphvah	Thunderbolt Half Lotus		Window/Door Frame Cornice, String Course
Bilari	String Flower		Pillar, Jamb
Bhujipa	Bell (Lit fly wing)		Window/Door Frame
Malaygvah Malah	Black Pepper dragon		Projecting ends of sill & lintel
Meymikha Mhayka Mhaykhapa	Buffalo Eye Peacock Peacock Wing	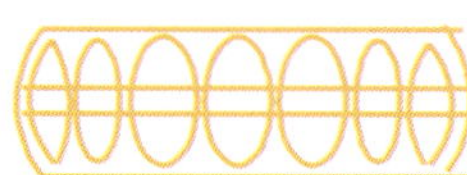	Pillar Pillar, Window

Bibliography

- Bernhard Kậlver, 1996 — **Constructing Pagoda According to Traditional Nepalese Drawings** Akademie Verlag, Berlin
- Banerjee, N.R. 1980 — **Nepalese Temple Architecture** Agamkala Prakashan, Delhi
- Chandra Bahadur Joshi 1988 — **Kathmandu Upatakaka Kalatmak hyalharu** Publisher: Royal Nepal Academy Kamladi, kathmandu, Nepal
- Dhurba K. Deep — **Popular Deities, Emblems & Images of Nepal,** Nirala Series-25
- Dr. Paisal Dahal — **Art & architecture of Nepal** Publisher: M.K. Publishers and Distributes Bhotahiti, Kathmandu
- Dr. Jagadish Chandra Regmi — **Shahakalin Kala Ra Vastukala** Publisher: Sajha Prakashan Kathmandu, Nepal
- Erich G. Theophile & Rohit K. Ranjitkar 1992 — **Radha Krishna Temple** Kathmandu Valley Preservation Trust
- Gerard Toffin 1981 — **Man and His Houses in the Himalayas,** Sterling Publishers Private Limited, New Delhi
- Gutschow and Kolver 1975 — **Bhaktapur** Kommissions Franz Steiner Gmbh Wiesbaden/BRD
- Gehendra Man Amatya 1998 — **Religious Life in Nepal** Publisher: Amatya Publishers Kathmandu, Nepal
- Gậtz Hagmậller — **Patan Museum The Transformation of a Royal Palace in Nepal,** Serindia Publications London

- Giovanni Scheibler 1982 — **Bhaktapur Nepal**
  Zurich
- Jnan Bahadur Sakya 1989 — **Short Description of gods, goddesses and ritual objects of Buddhism & Hinduism in Nepal**
  Publisher: Handicraft Association of Nepal
  Kathmandu, Nepal
- John Sanday 1979 — **Monuments of Kathmandu Valley**
  Unesco Paris
- John Sanday, 1982 — **Kathmandu Valley, Nepalese Historic Monuments in need of Preservation,**
  Unesco
- Jeff Lidke — **Vishvarupa Mandir**
  Nirala Publication
- Leela Row Dayal — **Bhaktapura Ratnam**
  Publisher: Gulab Vazirani
  New Delhi
- Mary Rubel, 1968 — **The Gods of Nepal**
  Published by BhimRatna
  HarshaRatna,Keltole Kathmandu
- Majupuria, 2006 — **Gods, Goddesses & Religious Symbols of Hinduism, Buddhism and Tantrism.**
  Publisher: M.Devi, Gwalior, India
- Mohan Prasad Dahal — **Nepali Kala**
  Publisher: Sajha Prakashan
  Kathmandu, Nepal
- Mehrdad Shokoohy & Natalie H. Shokoohy, 1994 — **Kirtipur : An urban Community in Nepal,** Araxus, South Asian Series
  London
- Mary Shepherd slusser 1998 — **Nepal Mandala,**
  Princeton University, Princeton,
  New Jersey.
- Niels Gutscow and Erich Theophile 2002 — **The Sulima Pagoda**
  Publisher: The Kathmandu
  Valley Preservation Trust
- Niels Gutscow, Bernhard Kolver & Ishwaranand Shresthacarya 1987 — **Newar Towns & Buildings**
  Hans Richarz Publikations Services,
  Sankt Augustin Printed in Germany.
- Percy Brown — **1912Picturesque Nepal,** London
- R.S.Gupte 1972 — **Iconography of the Hindus, Buddhists and Jains**
  Publisher: D.B. Taraporevala Sons & Co. Pvt. Ltd. Bombay

- Rishikeshab Raj Regimi 1993 — **Kathmandu, Patan & Bhaktapur**
  Nirala Publications, Jaipur
- Ronald M. Bernier 1970 — **The temples of Nepal**
  S.Chand & Company Ltd. Ram Nagar
  New Delhi.
- Ronald M. Bernier 1979 — **The Nepalese Pagoda**
  S.Chand & Company Ltd. Ram Nagar
  New Delhi.
- Sudarshan Raj Tiwari 1988 — **Tiered Temples of Nepal**
  Publisher: Mrs. Sunita Tiwari
  Kathmandu, Nepal
- S.B.Dao 1965 — **Glimpses of Nepal Woodwork**
  The Journal of the Indian Society of
  Oriental Art, Calcutta
- U. Wiesner 1978 — **Nepalese Temple Architecture**
  Leiden E. J. Brill
  The Netherlands
- Wolfgang Korn 1976 — **The Traditional Architecture of the Kathmandu valley**
  Bibliotheca Himalayica
- Wendy Moore — **Kathmandu** The Forbidden Valley,
  Time Books International, New Delhi
- Yadi Ratana Bajracharaya 2004 — **The Gunakar Mahavihar**
  Gunakar Mahavihar Conservation
  Committee, Jytha, Kathmandu
- Yadi Ratana Bajracharaya 1999 — **Artistic Heritage of Nepal**
  Publisher: Handicraft Association of Nepal
  Kathmandu ,Nepal
- Yogeshwar K. Parajuli 1985 — **Experiences in preservation and restoration in a Medieval Town**
  Publisher: Bhaktapur Development
  Project, Kathmandu